Savannah
and Pubs

David Harland Rousseau
and Dow Harris

Illustrated by
Julie Collins Rousseau

Pubs reviewed by
David Harland Rousseau

Schiffer
Publishing Ltd

4880 Lower Valley Road, Atglen, PA 19310 USA

Dedication

Here's to her who halves our sorrows
and Doubles our joys.

Disclaimer

Published by Schiffer Publishing Ltd.
4880 Lower Valley Road
Atglen, PA 19310
Phone: (610) 593-1777; Fax: (610) 593-2002
E-mail: Info@schifferbooks.com

For the largest selection of fine reference books on this and related subjects, please visit our web site at
www.schifferbooks.com
We are always looking for people to write books on new and related subjects. If you have an idea for a book please contact us
at the above address.

This book may be purchased from the publisher.
Include $3.95 for shipping.
Please try your bookstore first.
You may write for a free catalog.

In Europe, Schiffer books are distributed by
Bushwood Books
6 Marksbury Ave.
Kew Gardens
Surrey TW9 4JF England
Phone: 44 (0) 20 8392-8585; Fax: 44 (0) 20 8392-9876
E-mail: info@bushwoodbooks.co.uk
Website: www.bushwoodbooks.co.uk
Free postage in the U.K., Europe; air mail at cost.

Other Schiffer Books by David Harland Rousseau
Savannah Ghosts: Haunts of the Hostess City -- Tales that Still Spook Savannah

Other Schiffer Books on Related Subjects
Savannah Ghosts: Haunts of the Hostess City -- Tales that Still Spook Savannah. David Harland Rousseau.
Savannah Spectres. Margaret Wayt DeBolt.
Savannah Squares: A Keepsake Tour of Gardens, Architecture, and Monuments. Rob Hill.
Greetings From Savannah. Tina Skinner, Mary Martin, & Nathaniel Wolfgang-Price.

Designed by Mark David Bowyer
Type set in Benguiat Bk BT / Dutch 809 BT

ISBN: 0-7643-2530-2
Printed in China

Contents

Preface

"Everybody should believe in something. I believe I'll have another...."

Unknown

Think about the last time you were at a bar where someone regaled the crowd with some tall tale. Sure, you may dispute a fact or two, but there was something in the telling that made you sit up and listen. When all was said and done, it was a damn fine story, and one you probably shared at the office the next day. It didn't matter that it wasn't *your* story, because you had the complete attention of everyone standing around the water cooler. You may have even embellished the tale — just a little.

The very telling of the tale forges a legend.

Savannahians, like all Southerners, love legend. If we don't have one on the tip of our tongues, we'll make one up. Fortunately, Georgia's First City has more than her fair share of memorable myths — and they're all true.

Savannah Tavern Tales quenches the thirst for local legend by reintroducing a folktale with perspective and context. In the interest of good storytelling, corners were rounded, timelines compressed, and minor characters and events were blended together.

These tales represent the *zeitgeist* of Savannah. They're yarns spun around the pubs and taverns since the city's founding and span the life of the Hostess City. Dow and I encourage you to share these stories, toasts, and recipes with your friends back home — even if you have to embellish (just a little).

Sláinte!

David Rousseau
Savannah, Georgia, 2005

PS: For those of you eager to belly up to the bar, turn to the latter half of the book, *Pubs Review*. There, you'll find a survey of Savannah's favorite watering holes, all conveniently located within the Historic District.

PPS: History buffs may want to take a peek at the extensive bibliography found at the end of the book — a rarity for a collection of short stories, to be sure!

Acknowledgments

The authors would first like to thank M. Hilton Swing, president and founder of The Savannah Walks, Inc., who has always been a good friend.

The authors would also like to thank Savannah's tour guides, who keep the spirit alive (no pun intended) by telling and re-telling the tales to new audiences nightly.

The authors would also like to raise a glass to every barkeep who knew not only how to mix a mean drink, but who also knew how to spin a yarn.

Dow would like to thank Britton Elliott for all of her love and support. None of this would be possible without the inspiration that she gives on a daily basis. Dow would also give thanks to his parents, Bonnie and Mike Harris, for offering some great suggestions and encouragement. Thanks to Nova Thriffiley, a true New Orleans literary intellect of the highest caliber, for her excellent criticism and close-reading analysis. Dow would also like to thank David Rousseau for giving him the opportunity to work on this project and for rising to the occasion, as men must do. Finally, Dow would like to thank all of his friends out there who took time out of their busy schedules to read what he had written.

David would like to thank Mike and Cindy Hagan for their constant support and friendship for more than a quarter century, and who unflinchingly indulged him in his nonsensical flights of fancy, which have finally paid off. David would also like to thank Dow Harris for his challenging and engaging views, and for being the epitome of the Southern Gentleman.

Julie would like to thank Trisha Albano for her tireless support — and for a first-rate mojito. Julie would also like to thank Larry and Angela Williamson for their un-wavering love, tasty barbecue, and great conversations on the back porch.

"No Stamps, Gentlemen!"

David Harland Rousseau

November 1765

Ting!

The heavy playing card ricocheted off the lip of the spittoon and fluttered harmlessly to the deck of the ship.

"Bollocks," blurted Webster, more out of boredom than frustration. It had finally come to pitching cards. On the other side of a withering tower of rice-filled sacks, Webster could hear Mulligan singing a little ditty.

"Remember, remember the fifth of November," went the tune. Lyrics mumbled into a hum, and the hum feathered itself into a whistle.

Webster couldn't believe his ears. Was it already Guy Fawkes Day? Had they been stuck at port this long? He whipped another card at the spittoon, then another. Quickly, he snapped two or three more and then finally hurled what remained of the deck in the general direction of the brass bucket. He snatched his bottle of rum and stumbled to his feet. He kicked the spittoon hard, sending it headlong into the stacks of sacks. And with that, he headed topside.

As he yarded open the hatch, he bumped into Donnie Banks. Donnie was an easy-going bloke who seemed to find the humor in any damned thing. It was that affable nature that kept the crew from tossing him overboard months ago.

Webster gave the lad a nod and staggered up the steep steps. Donnie turned on his heels and followed Webster topside.

"Do you think they'll let us ashore to celebrate the holiday?" said Donnie, with eager anticipation in his voice.

"Who knows?" barked Webster. "I'm just hoping they'll let us off the bloody ship."

A week before, on the anniversary of the accession of King George, an unruly mob of Yanks had burned an effigy of a stamp officer. But Webster and the rest of the crew could care less about the king, or about the Yanks. They just wanted to unload their cargo and set sail.

As Webster leaned over the rail, bottle in hand, he thought about the ridiculousness of this newly passed Stamp Act. Every bloody document, from marriage licenses to bills of laden, had to be stamped — for a fee, of course. Problem was, there were no stamps to be had, since the ship carrying the stamps, H.M.S. *Speedwell*, had yet to arrive in port.

"I see no reason why gunpowder treason should e'er be forgot." Mulligan's baritone voice rolled over the deck planks like water from an overturned bucket.

"Bloody shame about the 'oliday, eh Mulligan?" grumbled Webster.

"Ah, we'll find some way to celebrate it," said Mulligan. "Even without fireworks or a bonfire."

"Guy Fawkes. Now there was a character," said Webster, taking a swig. "I'm startin' to think he had the right idea, wantin' to blow up Parliament an' all. I'd like to blow up Parliament me-self, what with all this rice rotting in the hold."

"Easy, mate," said Mulligan.

"Man's got a right to speak his mind, I should think," said Webster, gesturing with his bottle.

"Yer soundin' like the bloody Yanks, now," said Mulligan. He snatched the bottle from his frowning friend and took a couple of gulps.

"Might as well drink up," said Webster, slumping against the deck rail. "Nothin' better to do."

For the better part of the afternoon, Mulligan, Webster, and Donnie shared the bottle and sang bawdy songs. Every once in a while, Mulligan would make up a chorus or two about Guy Fawkes, which Webster would parody.

"If you haven't got a stamp to-day, then God bless you!"

Suddenly, Donnie jumped to his feet and shouted (to no one in particular), "No stamps, gentlemen!" Webster and Mulligan responded in kind by raising their bottles and, in their best Parliamentary voices, grumbled, "Here, here!"

"Where d'you s'pose 'e's goin'?" said Webster, watching Donnie stumble off to the Captain's Quarters.

"'aven't the foggiest," said Mulligan.

A few minutes later, Donnie burst through the door, wrestling with a rather grotesque effigy of Guy Fawkes. Mulligan and Webster stared at the spectacle. Then, they simultaneously frowned at their bottles of rum, as if the spirits were the cause of this comic vision. The young man tripped on a mop bucket, and he and "Guy Fawkes" tumbled to the deck. The oversized papier-mâché head bounced along the planks and landed in Webster's lap.

Silence blanketed the ship. Donnie glanced up at the two drunken sailors. Suddenly, Webster and Mulligan guffawed and chortled. Donnie collapsed onto the stuffed effigy with relief.

Webster lifted the oversized head and studied it carefully.

"Alas, poor Yorick!" slurred Webster, chuckling.

"A man of infinite jest!" snorted Mulligan. "Fancies that Punch character a bit more than Yorick, I'd say."

"Or Guy Fawkes, for that matter," said Webster. "But I'd bet 'e'd make an excellent stamp master!"

Mulligan and Webster snapped quick looks at each other, then at Donnie, then at the papier-mâché head of Guy Fawkes.

"No stamps, Gentlemen!" they said.

"Say it, Donnie!" said Mulligan.

"Loud as you can!" said Webster.

Donnie stumbled to his feet, straightened his tunic and bellowed, "No stamps! Gentlemen!"

Webster and Mulligan fell over, laughing at the boy's cracking voice. Donnie responded with a sheepish grin.

"Oh, the 'ell wif Guy Fawkes!" said Mulligan. "We've just created our own 'oliday!"

Word spread fast that Webster, Mulligan, and Donnie had something in the works — and it really must have been something for the usually stoic Webster to have a hand in it. Before too long, half the ship was corralled into their scheme.

It was a simple plan, really. The gang would fashion a rolling gallows out of whatever lumber they could find, throw a noose around the neck of Guy Fawkes-turned-Stamp Master and roll him around the streets of Savannah, all the while calling out, "No stamps, gentlemen!" Loyalists on the crew thought it parodied the rowdy Yanks, while others thought it a clever way to thumb their noses at Parliament's ridiculous law. The majority, however, were just suffering from cabin fever and needed some excuse to get off the ship.

As they put the final touches on the gallows (to include a hastily painted sign which read, "Stamp Master"), the crew hit a snag: they couldn't get the mannequin to sway from the rope. The straw stuffed body kept falling away from the head.

"Bollocks," said Mulligan. "We're sunk."

Webster, still buzzed from a bottle of rum, cradled the papier-mâché head and looked into the opening. Then, he gazed over his shoulder at Donnie.

"Donnie!" he shouted. "Think you can fit yer head in this?"

Donnie plodded over to Webster, bowed his head and let he and Mulligan slide on the mask.

"Move 'round a bit," said Mulligan.

Donnie took a few steps, and then danced a little jig.

"Brilliant!" said Webster. "I think we 'ave our new stamp master!"

As the sun set, Webster and Mulligan helped Donnie onto a short bench. Then, they slipped a noose around his neck.

"You'll be alright, lad," said Webster. "We tacked the stool in place. Just don't fall off!"

Donnie beamed as they fitted him with the papier-mâché mask.

"No stamps!" Donnie's muffled cry was met with cheers from the rowdy crew.

At first, as the men wheeled the gallows along River Street, they were toasted and cheered. Judging from their ditties, half the sailors on River Street thought it was still a celebration of Guy Fawkes Day and cheered the men and their make-shift parade.

Mulligan called up to Donnie. "You're a hit, lad!" Donnie responded with quick double-thumbs up.

Soon, the gang made their way onto Bay Street and down Barnard. As they lumbered toward City Market at Ellis Square, a few Yanks hurled epithets at what they thought to be an effigy of the stamp master. The sailors grinned broadly — until one of the colonists pitched a rotting apple. Though it exploded harmlessly on the yardarm, the soused crew found themselves in a stumbling run as they hauled the rickety gallows through the marketplace.

Over the cobblestones they rumbled, toward MacHenry's Tavern on the southwest corner. Mulligan and Webster each kept a firm hand on Donnie's legs, to keep him steady on the now wobbly stool. Butchers, still in their bloodstained aprons, filed out of their stalls in the beef market to investigate the commotion. A few laughed and cheered at the sight of this ragtag crew and their rickety gallows. Most went about their business, grumbling about strange days.

The tipsy crew dragged the cart to a stop in front of MacHenry's. One by one — and led by Mulligan — they filed through the door, slapping backs and lauding a good night's work. Webster looked up a Donnie.

"Okay, Donnie-boy," slurred a breathless Webster, leaning on the cart. "Get that foolish mask off and join us inside fer a pint or two!"

As the door slammed behind Webster, Donnie struggled with the oversized mask. He tried to slide it off, but mask kept catching on the knots of the hangman's noose.

Donnie cursed and tried to punch through the papier-mâché. Suddenly, the stool gave way. Donnie dropped — hard. He tried to hoist himself up, but he couldn't reach the rope. The wonky head prevented the lad from reaching back. Struggling, Donnie gasped for air. He began to see fireflies dance before his eyes....

Oh, Donnie.

If any pub could claim bragging rights, it was MacHenry's. Conveniently located near the City Market, MacHenry's was said to be a property more valuable than the Governor's mansion. Complete with gaming parlors and seating for up to forty, everyone who wanted to quench their thirst — for ale, and for gossip, frequented this stately pub. In truth, the self-styled Sons of Liberty gathered here just a few nights before, vigorously debating the hotly contested Stamp Act. So, it came as no surprise to anyone that there might just be an effigy of a stamp master swinging freely from the makeshift gallows parked just outside.

"Brilliant!" said a rowdy pair of Yanks as they staggered into the tavern.

"What's brilliant?" said Webster, craning his neck over his shoulder.

"That effigy of the stamp master, that's what," replied the Yank. "Feels like the real thing, too!"

Webster, Mulligan, and the crew felt the wave of nausea wash over them. Without warning, they bolted for the door, spilling drinks and knocking down chairs. They burst onto the street and were met by the grotesque, grinning, papier-mâché visage of Guy Fawkes, swinging from the creaking gallows.

"Remember, remember, the fifth of November" — and poor Donnie Banks.

MacHenry's Tavern *was lost in the passage of time, most likely during the 1796 fire. Its importance as a meeting place for the* Sons of Liberty *was largely overshadowed by* Tondee's Tavern, *which once stood on the corner of Whitaker and Broughton, and by what is now known as* Planter's Tavern, *a cozy little pub in its own right, located in the basement of the house built for patriot James Habersham, Jr. Savannahians now know it as* The Olde Pink House Restaurant.

Whiskey Tea

Boiling Water
1 Tea Bag
1-1/2 oz. Whiskey (preferably Irish)
1 tsp. Lemon Juice
1 tsp. Sugar (optional)

In a mug, pour the boiling water over the tea bag. Let steep for at least 1 minute. Remove the tea bag. Add the whiskey and the lemon. Sweeten to taste.

Ah, nothing takes us back to the glory days of Revolution and Rebellion like tea (for those Yanks in Bean-town in 1773) and Whiskey (for those "Keystoners" who tarred and feathered tax collectors in 1791). Were it not for these rabble-rous-

ers, we would hardly know the joys of Bourbon (those Pennsylvania distillers "relocated" to Kentucky), or coffee (its popularity skyrocketed as a way of boycotting tea in the wake of the tax). So, why not simmer down with this relaxing nightcap?

Shanghaied at the Pirate's House

David Harland Rousseau

July 1766

John Barley cursed. He scraped the horse dung off his new riding boots, and cursed again.

He reached in his pocket and pulled out his watch. *9:30.*

"Hate my job," he said, mounting his horse with a grunt.

Instead of nursing a beer at his favorite tavern, he had to patrol the dusty streets, looking for curfew breakers.

I'm a policeman, not some overpaid nanny, he thought.

He knew the stakes were high. Over the past few months, rumors of an insurrection against the Crown were brewing.

His horse stopped under a lamp at East Broad and Prince Streets. Barley looked over at the tiny tavern at Trustee's Garden. Just a few years ago, the Crown held high hopes for this grand experiment. Mulberry trees were brought in and a filature was constructed just a couple of blocks away, all with the belief that the silk yielded would also yield a high return on the Trustees' investment. Now, the Herb House served as a haven for rogues and scoundrels — but at least they weren't those damned Sons of Liberty.

He yarded out his pocket watch, popped it open, and tilted it to catch the light. The flickering flame from the smoky lantern reflected off its face. *9:45.*

"Two more hours," he said. "Bloody hell."

His horse reared, just a bit.

"Easy, girl," he said, patting her neck. Barley squinted into the darkness, and saw two shadows dart across the street.

"We're gonna get caught," Oliver said, crouching behind a withered shrub.

"Naw, Oliver," Tom said. "We're just havin' ourselves some fun."

Tom handed Oliver a length of grape vine. "Now, take it!"

"I'm not so sure about this," Oliver said.

"Okay," Tom said, grinning. "In that case, you go first."

Oliver threw Tom a sidelong glance and then sprinted across East Broad Street, with Tom hot on his heels.

"Damn it," said Barley through gritted teeth. He spurred his horse. The mare trotted down East Broad to where Barley had last seen the men.

Oliver and Tom crouched near a cabin near York Lane, waiting for Barley to ride on over.

"I told you!" said Oliver.

"Hush!" said Tom. "I'll get his attention. You just pull that vine!"

Tom sauntered out in the street at the mouth of the York Lane like it was the middle of the day. He even took the time to chew on a bit of straw.

"You there!" cried Barley, his horse now at a canter.

Tom grinned broadly, then dashed into the lane.

"Now!" Tom said as he darted past his old friend. Oliver leaned back, pulling the grapevine tight.

Barley spurred the mare. Rider and horse rounded the corner at a gallop. Barley ducked to avoid a low-hanging branch, only to be snagged by the grapevine snare.

SNAP!

The horse galloped into the night alone. Barley stared at the moonlit sky. The sound of grown men giggling echoed in the alley.

"Let's get his horse!" cried Tom, running after the mount.

Barley rolled over onto his knees and used a fence post to help him to his feet. He stood up and was suddenly awash with vertigo. Barley placed his hands on his hips and shook it off. When the stars left his eyes, he looked down the alley in time to see the two rascals ride off in tandem.

Barley whistled for his mount. The horse barely acknowledged him. Barley hobbled down the lane to East Broad Street and limped north, toward the tavern.

The constable caught his breath against a lamppost just outside the inn. He could hear raucous laughter coming from the tavern, and it made him smile. He was sorry he missed the raunchy story that made the rowdy crowd laugh so heartily.

As he climbed the steps to the inn, the door burst open. A drunken deckhand stumbled into Barley's arms.

"Yerr b'yuteefoh," he slurred, just before he retched. Barley stared down at the mess covering his riding boots, and let the man fall in his own vomit. He reached in his coat pocket, pulled out a kerchief, and wiped off his boots as best he could, letting the soaked rag fall at his feet.

Barley stepped into the smoky tavern and looked around. A couple of sailors lifted their noses from their tankards, but quickly returned to their beer. Barley wedged his way between two burly dockworkers and leaned on the bar.

"Usual, John?"

"Yeah."

The barkeep pulled a draught and set the mug in front of Barley. "It's on me, John," he said. "You look like you been rode hard and put away wet."

"Been a hell of a day," Barley said, sipping his beer. He heard one of the dockworkers snoring loudly.

"This a friend of yours?" said Barley, jerking a thumb to the snoozing worker.

"Nah, man."

Barley looked at the other dockworker. "How about you?"

The dockworker shrugged.

"Good." Barley shoved the big man off the stool. The worker slumped to the floor like a sack of rice falling off a carriage.

"Whatcha been up to all day, John?"

"The usual," he said. "Herdin' cattle. Can't keep these bloody Yanks off the streets!"

The burly dockworker waited until Barley was about to sip his beer. As the mug reached his lips, the worker stood up, thrusting his shoulder into John's. Beer sloshed and splashed on his uniform. Barley sighed. He set the mug down and stared at what was left of his beer.

"Curfew breakers?" said the barkeep as he toweled off a mug.

Barley sipped his beer and nodded.

"Yep."

"Must be tough."

John looked over his shoulder. A man just couldn't be too careful these days — especially if he were a loyalist.

"Couple of those jackanapes heisted my horse," said Barley, trying to keep his voice low. "And right out from under me."

The barkeep laughed, but soon realized Barley was serious. "Sons of Liberty?"

Barley shot the barkeep a silencing glare.

"It's okay," said the bartender. "They tend to gather at Tondee's. You'll only find men of the sea here."

A British naval officer bellied up to the bar.

"How about a round for the constable?" he said, sliding a couple of doubloons across the bar.

"That's very generous!" The barkeep snapped up the coins.

The captain winked. "If you could just bring me a bottle of your finest rum!"

"Yes, sir!" said the barkeep. "Right away!"

As soon as the barkeep disappeared around the corner, the captain said, "There is a man over there that has been glaring at you all night."

Barley shifted on his perch. The captain placed a reassuring hand on his shoulder.

"Don't be so obvious, my friend," said the officer.

Barley craned his neck. As he did, the Brit unfolded a small paper pouch with one hand.

"Where is he?" Barley asked, talking out the side of his mouth.

"Over there. In the corner."

Barley slowly turned around. The Brit gently shook the powdery contents into the frothy ale.

"I don't...."

"It's probably nothing, my friend," smiled the Brit. "Maybe his day was as bad as yours!"

The Brit slapped Barley on the back and laughed heartily. Barley glanced at him, and then joined in. The jarring was just enough to mix the potion.

"Have you ever considered a life at sea?" said the captain. "His Majesty could use a few stout hearts like yours."

"I'm a bit of a land-lubber, I'm afraid," said Barley.

"Aww. Once you get your sea legs, it's no different from being on land."

Barley sipped his beer and scowled.

"Something wrong?" asked the captain.

"I fear I've gotten the bottom of the keg," said Barley, holding the mug to the light. The captain tried to keep his composure. If Barley tossed his beer, he'd have to find another way to knock him out, as he was out of the sedative powder. Just then, the barkeep rounded the corner.

"I've got your rum, Captain Longport!"

"Good!" barked the Brit. "Because I have a new friend!"

Round after round hit the bar, and the heavy glasses piled up along the rail. After a few shillings, the barkeep was more than happy to water down the captain's drinks, while giving Barley the stronger measure.

"I-I've always wondered what it would be like to sail the seven seas in the s-s-service of His M-m-majesty," Barley slurred. "Taking on the Spaniards at broadsides. I tell you, anything would be better than chasing down cur-r-few br-r-reakerss.

"This is damn fine rum-m-m." Barley held up his glass for another round.

"If I didn't have a wife and churrin, I'd say to hell with this bloody place and sign on with you!"

"You're too kind," said Longport, holding up his glass. "Cheers!"

"Cheerrrss," slurred Barley. He slowly lifted the drink to his lips. His eyes fluttered. Barley's head hit the bar. The captain lunged for the glass before it slipped Barley's grip. Too late, he watched as the tumbler tumbled over the rail.

Blast, thought Longport. *He'd better be worth every drop!*

He gestured to a couple of deckhands who hustled over to hoist Barley up and off his stool.

"Barkeep!" said Longport. "I think my friend has had too much to drink!"

"Looks like," said the barkeep. "Takin' him out for some air?"

"Yes," said the captain with a wicked grin. "It'll do him good!"

"It might be easier to take him through the rum cellar," said the barkeep, with a knowing gleam in his eye. "There's a tunnel that takes you straight to the river, where the air is cleaner."

The captain nodded his thanks and waved the men on.

The deckhands dragged Barley around the corner of the bar and into a slightly larger room. In the corner on the opposite side was the entrance to the rum cellar. At the top of the stairs, they changed their grip on Barley. One deckhand cradled him under his shoulders, while the other held the constable's legs tight against his own body. They trudged down the narrow wooden steps. Longport, clutching an oil lamp, led the way.

In the back of the rum cellar stood an iron door. The captain moved ahead and tried to move the heavy latch.

"Hang on, hang on," muttered Longport, as he set the lantern down on a tun of rum. He leaned into the lever. With a grunt from him, and the groan of metal on metal, the heavy door creaked open. The Brit seized the lantern, and stepped into the tunnel.

Captain Longport stopped dead in his tracks. He felt as though his heart would explode in his chest. There before him, lit by the smoky orange glow of the lantern, stared a hundred pairs of widened eyes — the eyes of slaves waiting to be sold at auction. The Africans called to him from the shadows, with tongues incomprehensible to his British ears. Quickly, the Brits hustled Barley past the moaning slaves chained to the dank walls.

Just a little further, Longport thought — no — prayed.

After a few long yards of stumbling over unseen and outstretched limbs and plodding through puddles, he finally found the door leading to the river. Again, the door was too heavy to open with one hand. Longport bent over to set down the lantern and was suddenly overcome with nausea. Something was foul — most foul. Was it the mold in the tunnel? The sweat from the writhing bodies chained to the wall? He crouched slightly and rested his hands on his knees.

Shake it off, old boy, he thought. *Almost home.*

As Longport lifted his head, he found himself staring into the vacant eyes of a dead man. The dreadful gaze and ghastly pallor told him all he needed to know: the African had died of fright. Longport had seen this once before, as a yeoman on a slaver ship. The Africans, terrified of being confined, sometimes went mad during the long voyage from the West Coast of Africa to the Caribbean. Apparently, Longport's prayers never to see such horrors again had gone unanswered.

The Brit leaned into the door, eager to leave this frightful place. Suddenly, he was aware that something was seeping into his boots. He dropped his head and felt another wave of nausea wash over him. It wasn't water they had been tramping through, and it wasn't mold or mildew in the tunnel, or sweat from the slaves. With no one to unchain these men so they may answer nature's call, the Africans had no choice but to relieve themselves where they lay.

Frantically, Longport slammed against the iron door again and again until it burst open. The cool night air washed over them as the Brits spilled out of the tunnel and into the shadows of the city walls. Never before had they been so eager to return to sea.

Morning came early for the crew of HMS *Carrick*. A long night of drinking never mixes well with an early morning departure. Still, the captain afforded himself the luxury of a smile as the schooner set sail.

Longport loved the meandering journey down the Savannah River. Soon, the bluff would yield to low-lying marshes and graceful hammocks speckled with blue heron. Before too long, they would sail past the cedar lighthouse, which marked the mouth of the Savannah River, and therefore that ambiguous dividing line between river and sea. Rising ninety feet in the air, the unadorned, octagonal beacon served her sailors well.

A deckhand ran up to the captain.

"Should I rouse 'im?" said the sailor.

"I should think so," said the captain. "We're out too far now. He certainly can't swim to Savannah!"

The crew laughed.

The first mate snatched a bucket of water from a deckhand, who had been busy swabbing the deck. He stomped over to Barley and dumped the bucket of water over the constable's head.

The filthy water felt like shards of breaking glass against Barley's face. He sat bolt upright. He quickly glanced around. Gone was his uniform; a pair of breeches and a tunic had replaced it. Barley patted himself down to see whether it was all just a dream, but the raucous laughter from the sun-baked men brought him to reality.

"Good morning," Longport said with a smirk.

Barley shielded his eyes from the scorching sun. The deck was a flurry of activity. Men scrubbed the deck and unfurled the last of the billowing sails.

"Is this a joke?" said Barley. "Put me back ashore right now!"

The crew laughed raucously.

"I should think the crew will do well with you on board," the captain said.

"You're the captain! You can order the crew to take me back!"

"I could," he replied. "But I won't. Instead, let me to be the first of many to welcome you into the British Navy!"

Barley stared blankly at the captain.

"You, my friend, have been impressed into the service of the King!"

According to legend, it took this Savannah constable more than two years to return to the port of Savannah, where he was promptly released from service.

The tunnels below Savannah still contain their mysteries, as does the now-famous Pirate's House on East Broad Street. It is said that Robert Louis Stevenson penned a good portion of Treasure Island *here, while recovering from tuberculosis. The comings and goings of the sailors who frequented the tavern were the inspiration for such colorful rogues as the infamous Captain Flint who, as you may recall, died in the upstairs room of The Pirate's House.*

Grog

2 oz. dark rum
3 oz. water

Into an old-fashioned glass with no ice, pour the rum and the water. Stir well.

Oft romanticized in song and shanty, this drink is highly over-rated. British Admiral Vernon was affectionately called Old Grogram *because he often wore a coat made of a coarse fabric called* grogram. *In 1740, he ordered the watering down of the sailors' ration of rum. The diluted spirit came to be called* grog. *It couldn't have been too watered down because the word* groggy — *that sleepy, hung-over feeling one gets from tossing back too much rum — can be traced back to* Old Grogram.

The Eternal Dinner Party

Dow Harris

Thanksgiving 1775

"We're lost."

"No, dear, this is the way. I'm sure of it. Trust me."

The Habershams came winding up a long meandering drive in a horse and carriage, making a couple of sharply acute turns. Mr. Habersham looked out the back window to make sure they had turned at the right spot but already the forest seemed to close in behind them. He was more nervous than he let on to being. The avenue was mazelike.

It was dusk. Folks had been arriving at Bonaventure for the annual feast periodically throughout the day. The sky was now a pinkish-orange that faded into blue along the visible horizon. There was a strange golden light casting a surreal glow through the forest.

Mrs. Habersham turned to her husband.

"You would think that the house would be visible at the end of the avenue."

"Have you not heard the story of these trees, dear?" His voice betrayed an apprehensive cosmopolitan lilt.

The lady shrugged. The sounds of the wilderness permeated the vacuum of his query. He explained.

"Well, the house was the gift of John Mulryne to his daughter Mary on the occasion of her marriage to Josiah Tattnall. Mulryne also planted a series of live oaks directly in front of the house in the shape of an intertwined M and T to signify the joining together of the two families. It wasn't just a single line, but a double line of trees so that they grew together at the top and created a tunnel path with several pleasant turns."

"So, we're winding down a leg of the M right now?"

"Yes, if I'm not mistaken, and the intersection with the T is just up ahead. We'll soon see the house."

"Oh, darling, ha-ha, yes, I do see another carriage just rounding the bend up ahead. It looks to be the Johnston's. This is the right way. What a bizarre ride!"

She pulled out a little pocket mirror to check her makeup and hair.

There was a good view at Bonaventure despite the thick foggy mist rising from the water. The grand neo-classical home stood on an excellent commanding bluff overlooking the Wilmington River. And there was also a nice breeze that came whipping through the live oak tunnels that permeated the property. Sometimes the wind whistled or shrieked, sounding for all the world like bald eagles on the hunt.

Some arrived by land but some made the commute over water in boats. Families from neighboring plantations navigated through the extensive web-like waterways that connected so many of the old homes to the sea. They brought all manner of special casseroles, fresh fruits and pies, wild game and fowl, and, of course, plenty of brandy, whiskey, rum, and wine.

The Negro slaves, lords of rhythm, carried musical instruments slung loosely over the shoulder for entertainment later in the evening. As the boats were approaching, the sounds of *a cappella* harmonies from the black pilots boomed across the water toward Bonaventure.

All roads of rural indulgence and entertainment led to Bonaventure. Those in carriages hustled down the labyrinthine avenue, finally lining up in the central cul-de-sac around the big tree with four to six horses apiece. A little dust got kicked up in the air as the party began to get underway and so the ladies waited a minute or two before exiting the main coaches and making their grand debut.

Initially, everyone mingled outside. Tattnall's catering captured everyone's attention. There were extraordinary ice sculptures on *hour' d oeuvres* tables and bars. Classic figures from ancient mythological times were melting slowly and glistening under the simmering sunshine, sublimating into the heavy humid sweet sticky atmosphere. There was something gothic about how the heat was deforming the immoveable bodies.

Ice was unheard of in these parts but a ship from Massachusetts had arrived earlier, carrying big blocks from Gorrie's icehouse. This occasion had turned out to be an expensive affair but Tattnall was known for going out of his way to show off his beloved home. It was his most valuable worldly possession.

As the party got under way, the Africans began tuning up their fiddles and banjos; some were tending bar. There were also a few Irish musicians out there and even a Scottish bagpipe player. The bizarre acoustic amalgam created a powerful echo underneath the arboreal cathedral. Overwhelming all noise, though, was the chatter of excited conversation permeating the grounds. There was talk of war in the air. *Revolution*.

Lexington and Concord had erupted a few months before but was it really possible? Everyone was in a state of disbelief. *Revolution in Georgia?* After all, Georgia was the Loyalist Milquetoast. Some were skeptical but many sons had already begun to trade banners and were talking with fire in their eyes and Patrick Henry in their hearts. The Habershams, the Jones, the Sheftalls, and others tried desperately to harness their disparate ranks.

There was word that a large group of "Liberty Boys" had come down from Massachusetts on the ice ship that Tattnall had ordered, to agitate and *"stir the men up."* Rumor was that these northern fellows were radicals. There had been issues with violence breaking out in some of the taverns in Savannah. A few families received threats in the downtown and several had even taken a short trip to see country relatives until the city cooled a little bit.

Paul Tubbins, a local merchant who was assisting Tattnall in bringing the Sea Island Cotton seed to the coastal regions of Carolina and Georgia, was in the midst of recounting a harrowing tale to a group of young ladies, as he gulped a glass of Madeira wine.

"See, lie-dees. It was lak this. We was a drinkin' and carryin' on lak men do an' sich. An' this ol' boy, John Hopkins wuz 'is name. Yeah, he 'uz a arr'gant Brit mar'ner...jist passin' through...He's drunker'n all of us. Didn't realize who's sittin' 'round 'im. Stands up on the bar and yells at the top of his lungs, *"DAMNATION* to American Liberty."

He paused a second and looked at the ladies. His eyes bugged out. They shuddered at the harsh language.

"Yeah, complete silence. Hopkins giggles a coupla' tah-mes and burps squeamishly. Thought he wuz bein' funny. Two men sittin' nearby push him down off the bar. Hopkins then scurries to his room upstairs, lockin' the door..."

"And then...what happened?" A little blond haired lady tugged at Tubbins' arm. He spilled a bit of his wine. Before resuming, he watched the liquid drip to the ground with a hint of sadness in his eyes. One of the waiters was right there, though, and before Tubbins was able to look back at the half-empty glass, it had been refilled. In another moment, he threw it down the hatch.

"Well...later that night...the *Sons of Liberty* met up. They all wore grotesque masks to cover their identities. They paid off the hostess, broke into Hopkins' room, drug 'im a kickin' and a screamin' through the city streets and over to Johnson Square where they had a waitin' fer the British gent...a cauldron of boilin' tar!"

This was just too much for the sweet ladies. They opened their little powdered mouths wide in awe.

"Dunked him up an' down...up an' down agin'...till he agreed to 'pologize for his rude comments."

"And did he?" A brunette with large breasts stepped forward. Tubbins lost his concentration for a moment, distracted by the woman's womanliness.

"Yes, goddamnit...wow...yes...he did. Then they pulled him out and covered 'im with goose feathers. Somebody, ain't sayin' who, put a big clump o' Spanish moss on his head. He looked lak a hag o' the night.

When he had calmed down a little, they poured him a glass of Madeira jest lak ahm drinkin' now, and gave 'im the opportunity to make another toast...which he did. This tahm wishin' the 'mericans the best o' luck."

A short woman with curly hair who had been a bit coy and suspicious till now, waited a couple of moments as Tubbins finished his story, and then spoke up.

"How do you know all of this, Mr. Tubbins?"

He winked. She continued, now more wary.

"I bet you could also tell us the story behind the royal governor's kidnapping the other day, too. Eh?"

"No, ma'am. You'd have to ask ol' Habersham 'bout that one. His boy Joseph was person'ly responsible."

Just then a group of men came galloping up on horseback. Their clothing was sparse and tattered. Governor James Wright was at the head of the group. Had he escaped? Or was his kidnapping just a rumor? The men dismounted and rushed up, conferred on the porch, and then the leader went into the house alone. There was a temporary hush as the crowd parted and awaited a report. With none forthcoming, the gulf closed and the chatter resumed, even more heated than before.

The sound of heavy boots on the heart pine floor in the long hall startled the lord of Bonaventure, Josiah Tattnall, out of an idyllic daydream. He looked up from a clump of white cotton in his hand in time to see his old friend, James Wright, step boldly into the dark study.

At first the men didn't speak. They just looked at one another. It seemed that Wright had reached his breaking point.

"What are you holding in your hand, dear sir?"

"White gold, James. We're going to begin planting cotton at Bonaventure next spring."

"There won't be a next spring, Josiah. At least not for us."

Tattnall gazed out the window.

"I will not let go of Bonaventure, James. It *is* my home. My son knows no other."

"Either you will call off this nonsense and begin making preparations to leave or Bonaventure will be wrenched from your grasp by force. God help your family."

"Like I said, sir, we will begin planting cotton next spring. I've just returned from the Bahamas where they cultivate a strand of cotton known as *Sea Island*. It has a longer thread, is easier to separate from the seed, and will surely take deep root in the highland fields surrounding the bluff. This is just the beginning. Cotton will one day become synonymous with the South. Mark my words."

"That fool's share in your hands is all you will ever secure..."

They looked at one another. Tattnall put the cotton boll in his pocket.

"So, I heard you got kidnapped." Tattnall changed the subject.

"Yes, but they harbor no ill will towards me, only the position of authority that I represent. I raised half these 'Liberty Boys' with my own hands and they still approach me with some level of trepidation and respect. I was released with the promise that I would evacuate. There is no refuge left in Savannah. The time has come for us to go. You've got boats. Let's make our arrangements tonight, sir, before other arrangements are made for us."

Tattnall turned to look towards the window. Then he walked over to the bar and poured a tall glass of scotch into two tumblers. He looked back at his old friend.

"Let's have a drink first. I've got two hundred people in my front yard. This party will go on. You might as well enjoy it with us."

He handed the Governor the glass, which he took with no small reluctance.

Tattnall raised his and smiled, waiting for the governor to meet his gauntlet.

"May the joy of this occasion never end!"

The dinner bell rang and the crowd began filing into the large house. Everyone looked for his assigned seat. The dining rooms were immaculately set. The main table in the central room contained sixty chairs. There were placards by each plate. As soon as people began sitting down the servers brought salad and fruit out. There were fresh apples, pears, apricots, peaches, oranges, grapefruits, figs, scuppernongs, blackberries, and strawberries three inches thick. These were complemented by basketfuls of pecans and peanuts that were passed around in large bowls. And then dark spinach and lettuce leaves, fresh oils and vinegars, carrots, tomatoes, and celery. All of the preliminary food was reputed to have come from Bonaventure's garden. And then there was the Madeira wine.

The English brought grapevine cuttings to Georgia during the first generation in the hopes that she would thrive as a winegrowing region, Savannah being located at about the same latitude as Madeira. For the most part, the early vineyards did not do well, but some of the estates had maintained the cultivation up through the opening of hostilities. And so it continued to be a popular favorite.

Everyone had already had a drink or two of it, but for the most part, the Georgia Madeira was being saved for the meal. A number of French, Spanish, and Italian red and white wines were now offered to the guests. The interchange and clinking of glasses sparkling in the candlelight made for an interesting acoustic and visual effect. Though it was unorthodox etiquette, the guests had been encouraged to go ahead and take their seats and begin the preliminary munching and sipping, as Tattnall was still conferring with the Governor.

The two men had another drink together. And another. Tattnall had partially won Wright over and had now begun spinning yarns to put the older man at ease.

"Do you remember, James, the situation with *The Tryal* back in 1758?"

"That was before I arrived. That would have been under John Reynolds' watch."

"Yes, well, it was during the Seven Year's War, of course, and there was much hostility between us and the French and Spanish in those days. They were burning a lot of the coastal plantations with the help of runaway slaves they had captured and bribed.

"*The Tryal* was an English ship outfitted in Savannah that was sent out to patrol the area. This was right before Bonaventure was constructed. I actually remember John Mulryne addressing me on one occasion about its relevance. It was because of the danger to the exposed coast that he had taken such pains to hide Bonaventure deep within the river and up high on a bluff. He meant for the estate to withstand attack."

"And what is your point, Tattnall?"

"Well, it's just that the French and Spanish are gone, sir. *The Tryal* drove off the marauders. And Bonaventure remains, tucked deep in the bosom of paradise." Tattnall smiled carelessly.

"It's not the French and Spanish that we have to worry about, Josiah."

Tattnall shook the ice in his glass hard, spilling some of the Scotch onto the ground.

"James, as the Scottish say, '*bluid* is thicker than water.' We are all British. This dispute will work itself out."

A glass shattered in the hall just outside the room. Both men rushed to check the disturbance. George, one of the black slaves was busy cleaning up a glass of red wine that had fallen off of his tray.

"George, how long have you been standing at this door?"

"Not long, suh. I just was bringin' you and the guv'nah some wine like we served the guests."

Tattnall looked at his friend. He thought he had heard something move behind the door several minutes before the spill.

"All right. Well, I guess we should join the others, James. What do you say?"

"Yes." James was pensive. As they walked away, he looked back at George, noticing a transient grimace pass across the black man's visage.

As Tattnall and Wright joined the party, the main course was being brought out. It was an extravagant duck and quail dinner, compliments of a Mr. Zachariah Winkler, whose estate stood on the Northwest side of the Savannah River, a few miles above the city. Winkler had a great tradition of preparing the fowl with a secret recipe of spices. As soon as the meat was sizzling and ready, it would be pulled out of the oven and immediately placed in large fanner baskets in layers between wet leaves that had been steamed. Then white clothes were sewn onto the top of the baskets to maintain the heat and also to prevent curious fingers from having a taste. The baskets had been rowed over and had arrived exactly at the moment that they were to be served.

Winkler went to considerable lengths to have the fowl properly presented and everyone enjoyed the show as the servants began to unseal the large baskets on trays situated around the main dining table.

About midway through the presentation of the fowl, there was a loud scream from somewhere in the back of the house. The door adjoining the dining room to the serving anteroom swung open and the butler came rushing in, knocking over one of the big baskets and sending the duck and quail inside sprawling across the floor. Tattnall was furious. He slammed his hands hard on the dinner table as he rose to meet the nervous man approaching.

"What is the meaning of this, Henry?" He glared at the man and gripped his shoulder.

"Suh, I have somethin' turribly important to tell you. You must listen before you get angry, suh."

"Not here in front of my guests. Come with me." Tattnall retained his tight grasp on the butler's shoulder and stepped into a back room to confer.

The chattering and whispering commenced in the main room and in the other adjoining dining areas. What was the problem? Had someone been hurt? What was the scream all about? A number of the men who were frequent regulars at Tattnall's parties thought it was part of a production. Tattnall was known for his good humor. He often staged theatrical events during the meals to make them more exciting. But this seemed real.

A few minutes later, Tattnall reappeared without the butler. He had regained his composure and was now wearing a large smile. The party fell silent as they awaited his report.

"Ladies and gentlemen. Do not be concerned. You all know that we love to put on a show out at Bonaventure. No one is hurt and Henry was just playing his part. We wouldn't have you go away without some surprise now would we? Before I explain further, though, I would like to suggest that we move this glorious feast out to the front lawn. It's a bit stuffy and crowded here inside and there is a cool breeze that we all ought to take advantage of. Let us proceed.

Though there was a sigh of relief, everyone was confused. Why set up such an elaborate meal only to relocate? What sort of prank was Tattnall perpetrating? Seeing as they were his guests, there was no choice but to do as he pleased them to do. Winkler was upset. He followed Tattnall to ascertain the meaning behind this shenanigan. The servants began hastily picking up the dishes, baskets, chairs and tables and removing the dinner out to the front. The guests helped in any way that they could and followed the procession. Some of the ladies were a little peeved at the effort.

The main table was placed underneath the large oak in front of the house. When the rest of the accoutrements were set down, everyone took their seat again. The duck and quail were served and the wine was poured gratuitously in an attempt to rectify the inconvenience. Again, everyone waited for Tattnall.

Finally, he emerged from the large oak doors of Bonaventure and walked confidently up to his place at the head with his back to the big house. He addressed the party.

"Ladies and gentlemen. Now for the big announcement you've all been waiting for. *Bon A Venture*: The Good Way. What a wonderful blessing! You have been coming out to celebrate life and the fruits of this southern paradise for many years now. We have enjoyed your company. You know that this estate is my *most* valuable worldly possession. I have given everything for it and have rested all of my hopes upon it and the land on which it stands. My dreams of the future lie with Bonaventure.

"But now, as we gather together for this fabulous feast, I regret to inform you that it will be our last. For Bonaventure is burning down and there is nothing that any one of us can do to save her!"

Tattnall had maintained his calm demeanor all the way until the last sentence and it was a moment before the dinner party comprehended what he had just said. Then there was a gush. Some people were laughing at what they thought was a joke. Many of the women took him seriously though, and began weeping. But all realized that this was no show when they looked up at the house and thick smoke and orange flames began curling over the back end, which up until that very moment had been completely invisible. Bonaventure was on fire!

"Since we cannot save her, we are going to continue with our meal and celebrate our existence and give thanks while we watch her go down. This will be remembered as the longest and most extraordinary feast of all time. Eat, drink, and be merry!"

At this point, many of the men stood up and yelled at Tattnall that he must do something. Some that remained sitting spoke to one another of his mental instability. What sort of lunacy could carry on so carelessly in the midst of such a disaster? James Wright sat quietly contemplating the man and the bizarre situation. Tattnall was putting on a show all right, keeping his cool while his cherished dreams were destroyed before his eyes.

One of the servants approached Tattnall very carefully. It was clear that though he was holding himself together, there was an enormous pressure underneath this facade.

"Suh, we forgot the candelabras. They's still inside. Should we retrieve them before it's too late?"

"That won't be necessary, John. The flames from the house will illuminate the dinner just fine. Now pour me another drink."

His glass was filled. He continued standing. Then he lifted the glass up high and turned to face the burning house.

"May the joy of this occasion never end!"

He took the entire liquid in one gulp and without pause slammed the crystal into the oak tree with such power that the sound seemed to reverberate through the entire atmosphere, compounding the explosion of window panes along the sides of the house, too hot to hold the heat any longer.

And so the eternal dinner party carried on throughout the night. The bonfire offered a bizarre backdrop to the strange merriment. Passions rose to an extreme level of grotesque debauchery. Glasses were filled, refilled, and then filled again. The amplification made a deep impression on the record of the world. And the party melted into an ancestral beauty.

When Bonaventure was nothing more than a bed of burning coals, Tattnall suggested that they make another toast, saving himself for last. The men stood up, made their toast, and crashed their crystal goblets into the large oak tree, putting their own permanent acoustic imprint on the bark. When it was James Wright's turn, he and Tattnall shared a few words as he approached the head.

"And what do you have to add, James?"

"I think you said it best, Josiah...."

He sloshed his glass of Madeira around and raised it high.

"May the joy of this occasion never end!"

Wright gulped his drink and smashed the crystal.

Tattnall smiled. "That's my toast."

"Well, you'll just to have to think up something else. The King is dead."

Tattnall's glass was filled one final time. He contemplated for a couple of moments, looking over at the tears in his son's eyes. Then he turned and raised it up in an odd manner, holding the glass with both hands as if it were the grail itself.

"Long live the King!"

Josiah Tattnall III would eventually sell the ruins of Bonaventure Plantation to Savannah businessman, Peter Wiltberger, of the famed Pulaski Hotel. Wiltberger intended to develop a public cemetery that would include the Tattnall family burial ground, which had been used by that family since 1794. The City of Savannah would eventually purchase the cemetery in 1907, and has maintained the grounds ever since.

Mulled Wine

Curled Lemon Peel
Curled Orange Peel
2 tbs. Sugar
1 tsp. Ground Allspice
2 tsp. Ground Cinnamon
2 tsp. Ground Cloves
3 cups Boiling Water
2 bottles full-bodied Red Wine
Brown Sugar to taste (optional)
Cinnamon Stick Garnish

In a large pan, bring water to a boil. Add the peels, sugar, and spices. Simmer for 10 minutes. Reduce heat. Carefully pour in the wine and heat until sufficiently warm. DO NOT BOIL the wine. Carefully pour into a sturdy punch bowl. Serve with a cinnamon stick garnish. Sweeten with brown sugar to taste.
Makes 18 5-ounce servings.

Mulled (meaning heated and spiced) wine dates back to the middle ages, when it was called Ypocras, *after the Greek physician, Hippocrates. In the days of Dickens, revelers would warm the punch by thrusting a red-hot poker into the mix. (If you value home and hearth, don't do this, lest ye suffer the fate of the Bonaventure plantation....)*

The Punch Lining

Dow Harris

Savannah 1819

"Granddiddy, 'fore I take a sip, what all's in this thang? It looks awful strong. I mean, it ain't apple juice. That's fer shore."

An old man in a ragged Continental uniform sat on the back porch of his house over on East Broughton Street, Savannah, Georgia. He was a veteran of the American Revolution. He had a large, translucent brown colored drink in his hand that he was swirling in slow circles. It could've been apple juice to someone who didn't know any better. Ice cubes clunked together between cherries bobbing up.

The man had a head full of white hair that poofed out under a big cocked hat. There were heavy wrinkles in the corners of eyes that looked like an eagle's claw when he smiled.

The young man who had just spoken, his grandson, sat on the steps nearby. He also had a glass with the brownish fluid. It was his first *real* drink. This was one of those "comin' of age" conversations. His grandfather was trying to explain the precarious balance between concepts of respectability and the manly imperative.

They had been listening to the parade on Broughton Street. President Monroe and Vice President John C. Calhoun had come to visit Savannah for the first transatlantic steamship crossing. Local boat enthusiast William Scarborough was the owner of the S.S. *Savannah*. It was the wonder of its day and the herald of a ferocious future, a manifest destiny.

After the parade had passed, the young man had grown curious about the origins of the powerful drink they were sipping upon. His grandfather happened to be a teller of tall tales and there were no simple answers. He tended to weave history and mythology together into parables, symbols that might one day be useful to the young chap. Sometimes it was difficult to understand what he was trying to get at.

There was also a chessboard between them. Periodically, one of them would make a move, take a sip, or continue the conversation.

"Quite potent, indeed, my boy. Course, it didn't start out that way. The women wanted us to remain on our best behavior. But we, being men, of course, by and by, added the necessary distillations, while the ladies were not watching. The punch gives us a second sight, of sorts, ignites a super spirit within. You'll see."

"A sixth sense?"

"Something like that."

He shook his glass again and then shot a quick wink at the fellow.

"But what is in the drink itself?"

"Why, the Chatham Artillery, boy!"

"No. The punch that we're drinking, Granddad!"

The old man nodded. Cannons boomed in the distance. He knew what the boy wanted, or rather, what he needed.

"Well, we came together during the Revolution. That is where we derived our fire, initially, from the Revolution. *Revolution*, son!"

Once again frustrated, the boy shook his head, knowing that his granddad could not be cajoled out of his roundabout method. So he played the game.

"What does *revolution* mean, sir? I mean, really. It seems a strange word."

His grandfather gazed off into the distance.

"According to Mr. Johnson, the word *revolution* signifies the movement of a celestial body in orbit." He swirled his drink 'round and 'round for emphasis.

The young man looked perplexed at this answer.

"Here, think of it like this," the old man tried to be more explicit.

"When there's nothing left to lose, that's *freedom*. We were desperate and wild. The frontier catalyzed a rugged individuality that the Old World could not quell.

"It wasn't until the strong men of the country began to feel the weight of oppression that a *revolution* formed to challenge the tyranny. A revolution was necessary to break the mold and reset the cosmos around a new axis of power."

"Men of the *country* — as opposed to the *city*?"

"Yes, of course. That's it." The old man laughed at the teenager's confusion.

"All right. Back to the punch. What is actually in this drink? The ingredients. The recipe. What *exactly* makes it so potent?" The boy repeated his inquiry, more impatient this time.

The old man leaned back in his rocking chair and as he began to tell the story, the contemporary world receded into a more rustic time. The wilderness crept closer. They both took a sip of the world famous *Chatham Artillery Punch*.

The geezer laughed back through the years.

"It had all begun with a man named Washington...."

He comes, the Hero comes....

South Carolina Low Country, 1791

"Look at the bald eagle!" Major Butler exhorted as he gently jostled his snoozing companion. But it was the piercing shriek of the bird that woke the man.

President Washington came to and peered out of the window in the carriage. A glint of sunlight shimmering off the water nearby caught his blue eyes.

"I... did not know that they flew near the swamps."

Washington was going south for a tour of Dixieland. He was thirsty for a drink. They had just crossed the Ashley River and the sight of so much water was intoxicating. It was hot down here, the cool Virginian reflected. Savannah was to be the southernmost point of the journey. Could it get any hotter?

Charleston was behind them and now they were heading southwest towards the river settlements with Georgia on the mind. The landscape of the low country was quite different from the hills of Mt. Vernon. It was swampy and sticky down here. There was a brighter tone to the green in the foliage. The honeysuckle and jasmine were blooming.

His mind played back through the key episodes of the Revolution. The country had been born. *But what sort of country?*

A nation? A federal republic? Both? *A strange experiment, indeed.*

His first term was well over half done. He had doubts about the possibility of a second. He was seriously considering stepping aside as he had done with the Continental Army. He could have secured much more power to himself had he been so inclined at the right moment. But he had to set an example for the future generations. George Washington would be a name that people would love to remember — a name signifying leadership, liberty, honor, and manhood.

The work of the Executive was much more cumbersome and awkward than leadership in the field. He tired of the job. He longed for a life of agrarian obscurity. So, time to go south. Time to take a break and think things over a bit.

After another stint of daydreaming through his own heroic episodes, the landing at Purrysburg loomed up, where they were supposed to be ferried across the Savannah River by a party of veterans. They reached the bank before the greeters arrived. There was a heavy fog rising from the river and the tall marsh grass, making it somewhat hard to see more than a few feet before one's face. He talked with Major Butler as they awaited their escorts.

"Sure is strange. This fog. The wilderness is strong down this way. It's palpable. What, indeed, is on the other side of that river, Butler? I can't see anything."

"Ah, Mr. President, it is impossible to know, as impenetrable as the future."

Washington nodded and reflected.

"Yes, as impenetrable as the future. Well, sir, surely our descendants will secure the vision."

"The foundation has been laid." Butler enjoyed these navigational turned existential conversations with *his Excellency*.

And then, piercing through the fog, the ferryboat was in sight. And what a strange sight it was. There were twelve veterans dressed in light blue silk jackets with golden frills, black breeches, white gloves, and tall black round hats with letters in gold around the hat saying, *"Long live the President"*. It was Captains Putnam, Courter, Rice, Fisher, Huntingdon, Kershaw, Swaims, McIntire, and Morris.

They sang the song *He comes, the Hero Comes* in unison as they chugged away with oars and poles. Between beats there were a few heave-hoes to punctuate the rhythm. Washington grinned. What a bunch of sincere yahoos, these fellas were. Damned Georgia Boys: there, for a fight... there, to have a good time... there, to laugh a good laugh... there, to get one's back.

In the front of the party a younger man stood on the bow as they docked in. It was Captain Morris, Harrison Morris.

"Mr. President, we have arrived to transport you across the river Styx." It was clear that Morris had had a few too many and had broken the Savannah ladies' strict prohibitions regarding sobriety in the presence of the great man.

"Don't worry, all arrangements have been made. But before we go, you must drink of the waters of Lethe so that you will not remember the subterranean journey that lies before you..."

He held out his hand to the right, expecting someone nearby to place a full glass in it. Nothing happened. His eyes got big and he turned backwards. Then he lost his balance and fell right into the Savannah River. When he came up he pulled himself onto the ferry, shaking himself like a wet dog.

"Where the hell is the drink, men? Did you forget to bring the punch?"

Courter leaned over and whispered into Swaims' ear. Swaims nodded. They apologized sincerely for Morris' debauchery while someone in the back elbowed him in the ribs.

After a pleasant but uneventful visit with Caty Greene, Nathanael Greene's widow at Mulberry Grove, the presidential party headed for the city of Savannah. It was about a seven hour trip from that point. Now they were traveling by land along the bank of the Savannah River. They passed a number of other river plantations with luscious fields of rice, hemp, tobacco, and even a little cotton. The Africans toiled in the distance.

They reached the city at dusk. Washington was immediately struck at how sandy the entire place was. Upon approaching Yamacraw Bluff, he saw a large group of people gathering to welcome him.

General James Jackson and General Lachlan McIntosh assisted him up the bluff. Colonel James Gunn also stood nearby.

Beyond these men was a group of sharply dressed soldiers. Washington approached the men immediately, saluting them with the utmost vigor. Some of them were visibly sweating. Washington was the closest thing to a god that they had ever seen.

"The Chatham Artillery, I presume." Washington spoke with the confidence of a commander.

James Jackson spoke for the group.

"Yes, these are the strong men of Georgia. Eternal vigilance is the price of liberty. They follow the legend of your example. Men, the guns."

A hand was raised. An order was given. To the north a series of cannons fired across the river towards Hutchinson Island. Twenty-six discharges.

A moment of silence….

The crowd began cheering.

Washington gritted his teeth, steeling his jaw.

"I like the sound of that. Perhaps I can add to the timbre. Butler. Show these hospitable men what we have brought."

Major Butler pulled a red silk blanket away from a large bulk that had been rolled up from the shore.

Two beautiful shiny brass guns glistened in the sunlight.

There was a hushed awe.

"I captured these guns from Cornwallis at Yorktown, men, when I sent that old son of a bitch packing —"

Butler reached for the president's shoulder, interrupting him.

"Mr. President, are you feeling all right? That seems a harsh —"

Washington shook his arm off, continuing his address. Butler was perplexed at the President's lapse.

"They are yours now. Perhaps if I ever come back through, you can greet me with them along with your own."

Everyone — Chatham Artillery included — was surprised at his forthrightness. They had heard that his manners were impeccable. *Must not be so hoity-toity in Virginnie, after all,* one of them thought.

Jackson reached his hand towards Washington with the measured reverence of a man of honor.

"On behalf of the men, we are most grateful for this kindness. How can we repay you?"

"Show me a good time. Let's have a drink."

Jackson nodded at Washington's casual familiarity but was a little uneasy. He wasn't sure what type of drink the President wanted.

The men ducked into Brown's Coffeehouse on Bay Street with the mayor of Savannah leading the way. A coffeehouse was safe middle ground, no doubt. The proprietor was notified beforehand of the visit. There were red, white, and blue ribbons draping the walls and the bar. Coffee and tea were immediately poured in thick mugs for all the men. A couple of them pulled hidden flasks and added some of their own special sauce, careful to conceal the indiscretion from *his Excellency*. They gathered in a circle around Washington. There was a bit of preliminary chatter.

"Gentlemen, it's Friday, May thirteenth."

Butler made a quick mental note. As a Mason, he understood some of the more occult implications of the date.

"Friday the thirteenth."

"Yes, indeed."

"So mote it be!" The men yelled out loud.

A series of signs were made dispelling any lingering superstition but a powerful gush of wind tore through the company from the still open door, blowing out the lamps on the tables. There were several hushed shudders at the apparent omen. The windows were already shut and the party was shrouded in temporary darkness. This provided additional cover for a few quick sips of the more profane libations still hidden in coat pockets.

"Well, what'll we have to drink on such a dark day, sirs?" Colonel Jackson asked rhetorically, trying to lighten things up and hoping that Washington might inadvertently give them a clue regarding his beverage preference. The men chuckled. One yelled out.

"Hell, anything's possible."

Washington remained silent, smiling easily, feeling once again a strange urge begin to overcome his sensibility.

At this point in the story the grandson turned to the old man who was now on his third drink. The man's eyes had taken on a very strange glimmer.

"Why is Friday the thirteenth such an accursed day, Granddaddy?"

After a moment of sipping deep and looking out through several different dimensions, he replied to the boy.

"Friday the thirteenth, 1307. That was the day that Jacques De Molay was burned at the stake by King Philip IV of France. He was the leader of the Knights Templar and they had been tricked into coming to Paris, seeking the repayment of debts owed to them. Philip had them imprisoned and all their belongings confiscated. It was part of a larger conspiracy that involved the Pope. A papal edict had been issued condemning the order as heretical."

"What does that mean?" The boy interjected again.

"They were accused of worshiping the Devil."

"Oh." His eyes widened. "Did they?"

"Son, any truth that bears witness against an establishment is perceived as a threat. Therefore, practitioners of such a truth are called devil worshippers."

"I see." The boy was still perplexed.

"Well, Jacques refused to yield up any of the secrets regarding the order's vast treasure stores and mystical relics of ancient power. He was wise to the machinations and had previously made preparations for their holdings to be dispersed on a series of ships sent to Scotland and North America under the supervision of Henry St. Clair. For Western Europe this was the order that would ultimately form into the Freemasons, an organization with which many of the founding fathers, Washington included, were associated...."

"Okay, okay. Back to the story, Granddad. They were in Brown's Coffeehouse about to give some toasts."

"Of course. Let me see now..."

When the lights returned, two dozen cups of coffee and tea were raised in the air as if on salute. Those who didn't have secret flasks looked nervous and taut. They sighed. One veteran stepped forward. Another opened the door and made a signal to the artillerymen who were standing across the way, manning the guns.

"To the United States – May they long enjoy freedom in peace!! We have won our independence, men. This is our day! The end of tyranny! The beginning of our SOVEREIGNTY!!!"

"Here! Here!"

The drinks were thrown back in unison.

The sign was given. The guns burst out again over the bluff. Thirteen states. Thirteen iron balls over the river. Friday the thirteenth.

It had begun. Another man stepped forward.

"To the Federal Constitution and its true friends and supporters. May it be the guiding harness for the future balance of our government. The abuse of power has no place in this land!"

"Here! Here!"

"Power to the people!!!"

"Hurray!"

The guns burst forth over the Savannah River again. *BOOM! BOOM!*

"To the Vice-President and members of the Senate. May the example of ancient Rome inspire our statesmen to the sublime ideal of the orator, of the philosopher king!"

"Here! Here!"

"Here! Here!"

BOOM! BOOM!

The President stepped forward. Everyone was silent. He raised his cup of Joe up, thinking of a harbor breeze and the Spanish moss on an old live oak. Something strange, though, had begun itching in his brain.

"To the commercial interest of Charleston! Savannah's older sister!"

There was a pause. The men squinted.

There was a bit of competition between these two awesome cities. Of course, Washington knew this and was intentionally seesawing on their good will. His task had been to unify them. It always would be.

"Here! Here!"

"Here! Here!"

"To Charleston. Yes. No longer is she *Charles's town.*" A robust man grinned at his clever quip.

BOOM! BOOM!

Washington scratched his head.

"I don't know. Yes, this coffee is nice. But, ah...." Then he thought of Martha. "Well, where'd you get the bean, after all?"

The men looked around at one another, also thinking of their wives. No one spoke.

Lachlan McIntosh made things easy.

"It's a brew from Colombia, sir. Slightly acidic. Ahem-hem."

A quick refill and the toasting continued. The conversation immediately became frenetic. The caffeine made everyone loquacious and argumentative. There was an animus present, looking for an outlet.

Colonel James Gunn was now standing near the President.

Washington turned directly to him. Gunn smiled in admiration.

"Colonel Gunn. I understand that you and General Greene did not get along too well. He actually wrote to me personally about this dilemma, seeking my advice."

Gunn closed his eyes briefly. The smile disappeared. This had been a sore spot but he could not unleash against Washington. No way. Had to keep cool.

"Yes sir. We failed to get along. To be honest, I resented his puritanical ways. I think that he wrongly made an example of me during the war."

Washington was open-minded.

"I'm sorry. You'll have to refresh my memory."

"It was over a horse I sold during the war to secure supplies. General Greene accused me of selling army property without the proper authority. He court-martialed me. I never forgave him."

"Did you not sell the horse?" Washington asked, now becoming angry.

"Yes, but it wasn't for myself. The times were desperate. Our resources were limited. It was a judgment call that I made out of necessity."

"To the contrary, it was in your personal interest, an interest that you valued above the greater good of maintaining the chain of command. You could've directly sought General Greene's assistance. Regardless. Greene was your superior — excuse me — *is* your superior. You should not have challenged him. Those repeated insults and threats that you threw at him and his family after the war *infuriated* me. To think that such a heroic man like Greene, beyond reproach, had to enter the city of Savannah armed with pistols lest he encounter your brash temper. How could we possibly maintain the proper relationship fundamental to military command structures and ultimately to civilization, if a subordinate officer such as you were able to overthrow the authority of a general out of a mistaken sense of honor? We would have chaos. No, you were in the wrong, Colonel Gunn. I'm sure of it. Greene's refusal to duel was not out of cowardice. He had long ago proved himself in that regard. I promise you that. Do you not remember Cowpens, Kettle Creek, King's Mountain, and Guilford Court House? Greene's courage, not yours, saved the South."

Gunn was aghast.

Colonel James Jackson looked across the room and caught a glimpse of the poor man's dilemma. He walked over.

"President Washington, may I have a word with you for a moment, sir? Let's go to the bar. It looks like you need another refill."

Washington's temper was hot. He had been meaning to confront Gunn over this matter. His eyes took on a glow of intensity. This was the side of the man that the British had come to fear.

Now James Jackson himself was a force to be reckoned with, too. He was a shorter man, known as the "fighting pygmy" due to his inclination for dueling. He was one of the early Masonic leaders of Georgia. He had the unique characteristic, like Washington, of sublimating his ferocious instinct into an inspirational leadership. During the war, he had been part of a successful foray smuggling powder off of British ships anchored in the Savannah River. After the city had been seized in December of 1778, he had fled up to South Carolina and joined with larger regiments to reassess. He had distinguished himself at King's Mountain, Kettle Creek, and Cowpens, as well as dozens of other smaller skirmishes.

After the war the state Legislature of Georgia had asked him to serve as first Governor. He was thirty. He declined, citing youth and inexperience. A man with such ambition as his was rarely capable of such a resignation. But Jackson was genuinely interested in the welfare of Georgia. And though he loved to fight, he was also a peacemaker, especially amongst good friends or citizens.

Washington continued to stare straight at Gunn for a moment or two more, and then followed Jackson to the coffee bar. They sat down.

"Are you feeling all right, sir?"

"Yes, of course." He shook his fist at Gunn and showed his teeth. Then he looked back at Jackson and changed the subject.

"So the Brits really held onto Savannah as long as they could, didn't they?"

Jackson saw where it was going.

"Yes, they did. They didn't call Georgia *the Loyalist Milquetoast* for nothing. The Tory element was very strong here. We had much more to kick against."

"But you were the first to reclaim the city?" Washington queried.

"Well, to be honest Mr. President, I have to give that honor to *Wayne!* It was his army."

Jackson turned his voice up, knowing that Wayne was nearby. Unfortunately these men had fallen out of sorts with one another due to a post war political rivalry and some dishonest electioneering by one of Wayne's campaign managers. The tragedy of it was that Wayne had been innocent of the corruption. Jackson therefore really didn't hold anything against him. "Mad Anthony" looked up for a moment and grinned, tipping his hat. Washington called over to him.

"General Wayne. I hear you've been spending a lot of time calling on Caty Greene, providing her comfort during her time of mourning over the passing of Nathanael." Washington had a way of piercing to the heart of the matter. Caty was very popular with all of the men and even more so after her husband's unexpected passing.

Wayne turned a dark crimson. The Yankee nodded his head and turned away, taking a long cool sip on his hot coffee. He burned his tongue but didn't let on to the pain. He motioned to the waitress, making the secret sign for the additional kick to be slipped into his drink. It was hard to look the tall Virginian in the eye.

"It was Wayne's army," Jackson continued, "but it was I who *led* the expedition into the city. We finally forced the Brits out. All I could think about, though, as we marched in, was the miserable rash between my legs. I was walkin' like a sailor."

Washington laughed.

"How did that happen?"

"Well, we were all wearing deerskin leggings like the Indians. When civilization fell apart, it was the wilderness that clothed us. We must have looked like scrawny barbarians walking back into Savannah in those days."

Washington had been watching Wayne's secret sign and when the waitress passed him, he tickled his ear and rubbed his thumb across his throat. In a flash, the young girl produced a small decanter and poured generously into his coffee. No one was any the wiser. Much better, Washington thought, draining the glass. He looked back towards Jackson.

"And Colonel, what of the formation of the Chatham Artillery?"

Jackson put his hand through his hair and scratched the back of his head.

"Well, really, the company is comprised of the men who defended Savannah and bled for her during the war. Most of us were just country boys before hostilities. We were all friends, had grown up hunting together.

"After the war, we were all well aware of the sacrifice it took to win our freedom, how precious it was. But even with the ceasing of hostilities, there were constant problems in the area. The initial euphoria of victory began to wear off especially in the rowdier quarters. Many of us recognized the importance of maintaining a degree of formal organization to prevent anarchy and the incessant internal and external disputes that inevitably follow the destruction of the establishment."

"Uh-huh, I see. Hmmm. Colonel, I think it's time for another drink."

"To the fair daughters of America!"

"Here! Here!"

"Here! Here!"

BOOM! BOOM!

The pretty young waitress was picked up and placed on a table. She grabbed an American flag hanging off the wall and waved it in the air. She looked out and could see all the men before her. They were all making the secret sign, desperately trying to get her attention.

"To the Secretary of State – may the important services he has rendered to the commercial interests of his country, endear him to every merchant."

"Here! Here!"

"Here! Here!"

BOOM! BOOM!

Jackson continued the thread.

"In June of '86, General Greene got the worst sunburn that anyone's ever gotten down here. He was bedridden for nine days. Doctors tried to bleed the fevers out of him using leeches."

Washington shook his head when he thought about that.

"And he died."

"It was a terrible occasion." Washington remembered, thinking of Caty, and how lonely she must be.

"So, the Chatham Artillery handled the funeral. We carried his coffin over to Colonial Park. We shot our guns to honor him. Some of us even wept over his passing. Afterwards we came here to drink our punch, I mean, coffee, and recall his deeds of greatness."

After the thirteenth toast, the men were barely able to stand still. Most of them were shaking a leg, anxious to relieve themselves. This was not the kind of party they had been hoping for. Brown's Coffeehouse was a commotion. Washington silently stepped outside to smoke a pipe.

Upon discovering his retirement, the rest of the veterans and city luminaries still inside came together for one final toast. This time bottles of whiskey were brazenly brandished. But Washington was still a mystery and no one had gotten a clue as to what he really wanted to drink.

"To the illustrious President of the United States! Long may he live to enjoy the praises of a grateful people!"

"And to his lady!"

"Here! Here!"

"Here! Here!"

BOOM! BOOM!

General Lachlan McIntosh slipped out, seeing Washington through the window.

"Sir, would you like to see the field where the battle of Savannah was fought, before nightfall?"

Washington turned to meet him.

He nodded.

"That would be fine."

His voice dropped to a whisper.

"And maybe you could tell me, Lachlan, where one could get a man's drink round this place?"

The Scottish Highlander paused for a moment, surprised at the admission. Then tapped his coat pocket, smiled, and winked at the Prez. He had a pint of Scotch and he wasn't afraid to share it, despite the game that the other men were playing.

They walked over towards Franklin Square and then turned left and headed to the Spring Hill redoubt where the American forces had made their attack on the British lines of defense on October 9, 1779. When they were out of sight, Lachlan passed the pint to George, who guzzled down two shots in one gulp. Said he had some catching up to do.

As they walked in a not so straight line, Washington queried McIntosh about his situation with Button Gwinnett, one of the more respectable signers of the Declaration of Independence from Georgia.

"Well, it was lak this," McIntosh began, his thick brogue rumblin' forth. "I was in charge of the troops in Georgia at the time. Bulloch, who's actually the first "President" of the state, had died not long after he was elected. Gwinnett filled the vacancy.

"And I didn't like him too much. He was a civilian, a shop-owner in downtown Savannah, and, in my estimation, a damned coward. He wanted to control every aspect of the militia's movements down into Florida. Course, he had no idea what he was getting involved with and he failed miserably to achieve anything down there."

Washington grabbed the flask from McIntosh. They were fast friends again, just like during the war. McIntosh grinned and then continued.

"Gwinnett's failure led to further resentment of me because I had pressed him that he should let me lead the troops. A few months later he came back at me, accusing my brother George of treason."

"Your brother's name is George, too?"

Washington laughed at the absurdity. He knew firsthand about McIntosh mettle. McIntosh grabbed the pint back and took another deep drag.

"Yeah, just like you, ol' Georgie-peorgie, 'cept he's not as famous. But back to me and Button....

"Of course, Gwinnett's accusation was a straw man. It was completely groundless. George had already horsewhipped Walton, one of the other signers, for making a similar accusation about me.

"So I called Button Gwinnett 'a damn scoundrel and a lyin' rascal' to his face next time I saw him and he just couldn't stand it. Challenged me to a duel.

"We met the next morning. We stood at twelve feet apart, facing one another. I had actually requested nine. Then we shot each other. I took a hit in the leg but I remained standing. His knee was dislocated and he fell down. He died from the infection three days later."

Both men drained another shot. Now, it seemed they were floating through the city.

The field where the Battle of Savannah had taken place loomed up ahead. It was now grown over with weeds. Some of the old redoubts, fortified stone piles, and fencing were still there but it was a bit hard to make out how things had been. Of course, now, they had a little help from the spiritual world.

"You were there, Lachlan?" George asked, pointing to a large pile of horse manure.

McIntosh appreciated the joke, doubling over and laughing so hard he choked.

"Uhhh.... I was actually there, sir. At this point." He stood beside a young oak tree and took a good long leak directly on the bark.

"I could make it no further. In one hour a thousand men fell on our side. It was terrible. We had waited too long to attack. John Maitland's bagpipe regiment saw us. There was no surprise, as we had originally intended. We were forced to retreat before noon."

He passed gas and Washington had to move back a couple of steps till it dissipated. McIntosh laughed again and then continued.

"It was a circus of a time, though, and I look back on it with fond memories despite the defeat. Haitians, Poles, French, and of course, us. There were a bunch of guys down from Carolina, too: William Jasper, Francis Marion, Charles Pinckney.

"Polish Count Pulaski was a real character. Talk 'bout a boy who could hold some liquor. Fellow dressed in bright clothes all the time like a rooster. Was always doin' horse tricks. He had one where he would stand on his horse while at full gallop and aim his pistol at a target out front. The guy never missed. But he offered too flamboyant a target for the British fusiliers to pass up. He got nailed right between the legs."

Washington cringed when he heard that. He eased the pain with another shot of scotch. *Had to hurt. Had to hurt.*

"And what of Jasper? Where did he fall?" Washington turned and walked forward several yards trying to envision the fire of battle and the fatal charge.

McIntosh continued after sucking the half empty bottle. Both men were becoming dizzy as they saw ghosts and supernatural cannon fireballs launching up from the battlefield.

"I never seen a braver man in my life. He fell further up." McIntosh approached a small mound of rocks that had been used to mark the spot, tripping in a drunken stupor. He picked himself up, dusted off his stomach, and posed as if he was holding up the flag. Jasper had gotten within five yards of the redoubt. McIntosh hiccupped.

"Are you meaning to tell me, sir, that Willy ran this far up to the British cannon before he was hit?"

"Yes, Mr. President, he did. He made it farther than anybody else. In one hand he carried the flag of Carolina, in the other he had a sword. He died fighting like a man."

"The best any man can ask for." Washington whispered silently to himself, patting his heart, looking for his pipe again.

"You know Jasper's name was already famous by that time for saving the colors at Ft. Moultrie in '76."

"I know." Washington rejoined, lighting up and sucking hard on the Virginia tobacco he had concealed from Martha. She warned that it was making his teeth yellow.

"The governor gave him his sword and offered him a lieutenant's commission —"

"Which he refused because he could neither read nor write," Washington finished the tale for him.

Night soon came on and they were forced to head back. They got lost in their drunken weavings but finally decided to follow the sounds of laughter and music from a northerly direction, towards the water. There was a big barbecue dinner under a massive tree arbor that had been arranged by the women of the city earlier in the day.

During the meal, the ridiculous toasting continued over tea and water. Again, the women of Savannah were responsible for the strictures regarding alcohol and they were making sure that things stayed that way. Martha, the President's wife, had sent word that everyone was to remain sober in his company. And she meant it. She was also worried about Caty Greene. She knew George was fond of the little lady.

The temporary prohibition had caused the Chatham Artillery great pain. But up until this point, they had maintained at least the appearance of respectability.

The party was situated on Yamacraw bluff at an angle with the river in view. All of the homes were brightly lit with lanterns. There were about 1500 people living in Savannah at that time but with all of the lights it felt like more. One house had an enormous "W" outlined with candles.

After the dinner got underway, fireworks began exploding over the river. One of the local ships had furnished this portion of the entertainment.

The band played some of the popular melodies of the day.

The dinner party proceeded directly from the table over to the old silk filature house on Reynolds Square. This was the biggest building in the city and where the silk industry had originated in North America. Solomon's Lodge No. 1 met in the building, but tonight it was reserved for dancing. A grand ball on Friday, May thirteenth, was being thrown in George Washington's honor.

Many of the men had been distressed about Washington's apparent dissatisfaction and boredom throughout the day but were relieved when McIntosh notified them of his intemperate retreat with the President just before dinner. The Chatham Artillery of Georgia got to thinking and finally came up with a plan on how to circumvent the women.

They convinced the ladies to make a fabulously respectable punch to impress ol' George. So, in the prep room, the ladies commenced to mix a tasty drink with exotic fruit juices and regional curiosities. They began stirring liquids into a huge vat. When they were done, General Jackson addressed them.

"Ladies, the President of the United States has been commenting on your beauty all day long but has lamented the fact that he has not yet had the pleasure of meeting each of you, individually. So I am here to ask you to now retreat to the powder room and prepare yourselves accordingly."

The ladies, flattered to say the least, left the prep room in a rush and went to make themselves ready. When they left, the Chatham Artillery filed in and gathered around the bubbling vat. They commenced to pour ungodly amounts of hard liquor and wine into the "respectable" fruit punch that had been left behind.

All in all, ninety-six Savannah belles, dressed in their finery, readied themselves to greet *the Man*. As each lady walked past the prep room towards him, eagerly anticipating presidential favor, a glass of the new and improved concoction was placed in her hand. She was to ask the President if he would like a sip of Georgia's finest, the Chatham Artillery Punch, and then curtsy and urge him to consume more.

Washington played along, catching the drift after his first taste. As each woman offered him a sip of her drink, he gladly took it, tried it piously, and returned an empty glass. By the time all ninety-six ladies had rubbed up against the first President of the United States, he was quite positive that he knew what the drink might be missing.

He cleared his throat and proceeded to make his own announcement:

"Ladies and gents of Savannah. Ah've *ther'ly* enjoyed me time here and ah've been drrrrrinking from the cups of all these brrrright young maidens, and thinkin' 'pon the ingredients of this wonderful Chatham Art'ery Punch — *burp* — of which you rightly boast...."

The President stumbled, almost losing his balance.

"What it needs, though... the missing ingredient — *belch* — What I want to see the most is...."

Everyone held their breath. This is what they'd all been waiting for, the President's secret desire.

"*Cherries*! Big, ripe, juicy, red cherries. *Heh heh. Yeahhhh!* Men, let us go and gather some cherries! *Whoooo!*"

All of the women blushed.

Washington laughed.

"I cannot tell a lie. Yes! Yes! A man's gotta have him some cherries."

Major Butler grabbed the President's shoulder.

"Sir, I think you may have had too much —"

Before he could finish, George Washington grabbed one of the ladies nearby and started dancing with her. It just happened to be Caty Greene, the widow of his best friend and most trusted subordinate. The Quaker Preacher General. But ol' Nathanael was dead now. *And after all, it was Friday the thirteenth.*

The old man snapped out of his trance and looked over at his astounded grandson.

"Granddad, what did that story have to do with the ingredients of the punch?

"You could've just told me that it had all these things mushed together. Besides, I already knew that it had cherries. I can see them floating around in the top!"

Poor boy. The geezer had generated at least three different angles with that conclusion and was already dreaming up others. But this was what coming of age was all about….

"Well, son, what you have to understand is that *men talking men's talk* is the ultimate ingredient. That's why we drink in the first place. Until you discover that, you have not understood the recipe of manhood."

He raised the glass one last time, and winked.

While most of the places mentioned in this story were lost to time, many of the present structures bear some reminder of those days of Revolution, such as Tondee's Tavern, the Silk Filature, and Battlefield Park.

Chatham Artillery Punch

1-1/2 gallons Catawba Wine
1/2 gallon Rum
1 quart Gin
1 quart Brandy
1/2 pint Benedictine
2 quarts Maraschino Cherries
1-1/2 quarts Rye Whiskey
1-1/2 gallons strong Tea
2-1/2 pounds Brown Sugar
1-1/2 quarts Orange Juice
1-1/2 quarts Lemon Juice

Mix from 36 to 48 hours before serving. Add one case of champagne when ready to serve.
Serves 160. (Bring some friends.)

The Chatham Artillery, organized on May 1, 1786, is the oldest military organization of record in Georgia.

During Washington's Southern tour, the Chatham Artillery saluted him with twenty-six volleys. They also toasted him with a heady concoction that was, shall we say, "enhanced" by the artillery officers, much to the chagrin of the gentle ladies who created the virgin version. It is, arguably, the most noted drink in two centuries.

Author's note: several restaurants in Savannah serve this potent potable, the Shrimp Factory and River House Seafood among them. I recommend NOT using a straw, as this punch packs a wallop. Also, a word about straws: If you want to show a true Southerner that "y'ain't from around here," use one o' them Yankee sippin' sticks.

A Fashionable Murder

David Harland Rousseau

January 1833

Robert Charlton parted the blinds of the courthouse and peered out the window. A small crowd was gathering in Wright Square. He let the blinds fall and reached in his vest pocket for his watch. With a quick jerk, the face swung open. Charlton pursed his lips and snapped the watch shut. He exhaled slowly and slid the watch back in his vest pocket.

"Should be any time now," he said. Almost simultaneously the other members of the defense team looked up from their dossiers, but just as quickly returned to their writing. If the case went south, they were ready to file an appeal.

Their client, Dr. Philip Minis, stared vacantly at his hands. He had held that posture since Judge Charles Dougherty gave his "lucid and impartial charge" to the jury.

He wondered, how had he, a prominent doctor and respected member of Georgia's First City, allowed a drunken braggart to get the best of him? He found it all so hard to believe that it all began with a simple game of quoits....

Spring 1832, Luddington's Pub

James Jones Stark wedged his way between the barflies holding court. Apart from exchanging perturbed glances, the men simply shrugged and took their conversation in another part of the bar. They knew better than to argue with a man who was known for his hot temper as much as he was known for toting a pig-sticker.

The barkeep set the glass of whiskey in front of Stark. Just as he was bringing the glass to his lips, he felt a firm slap on the back. Were his elbows not firmly wedged on the bar, he might have taken a swing at the gent. Instead, he calmly set down the glass and slowly looked over his shoulder.

"Wayne," said Stark. "You oughta know better than to sneak up on a man like that."

"Who said I was sneaking?" said Wayne, motioning to the barkeep. "Everyone here saw me make a bee-line toward you."

Wayne took the glass and gestured for a toast. The two men clinked glasses and downed the shot. They grimaced. As the glasses hit the bar, they exhaled and motioned for another.

"Quoits, huhn?" said Wayne with a smirk.

"You hush," Stark said, pursing his lips.

"I reckon that might have been the greatest ass-whoopin' in the history of the game," said Wayne. "Hell, I'm surprised you showed your face in here!"

"Ain't nothin'," said Stark. "That Minis is a damned Jew."

"Well, that 'damned Jew' schooled you at the Coits Club," said Wayne. "That's for sure."

Stark tossed back another shot as applause filled the room. He looked up to see Dr. Minis enter the room to a hail of handshakes and backslapping.

"Well, James?" said Wayne, grinning from ear to ear. "Are you going to offer your heartfelt congratulations?"

Stark slammed the glass down on the bar and wiped his mouth with his sleeve. "He ought to be pissed upon."

With that, James Jones Stark straightened his coat as best he could and ploughed his way through the crowd. Everyone expected fisticuffs. Instead, Dr. Minis calmly smiled and extended his hand. Stark refused the gesture and returned it with a menacing glare. As Stark staggered onto the street, he brushed against Dr. Arnold, who was waiting to congratulate Minis on his victory. Stark grabbed Arnold by the collar and jerked a thumb in Minis's direction.

"He ain't nothin' but a damned Jew," slurred Stark.

When Dr. Arnold finally reached Minis, he placed a hand on his good friend's shoulder and said, "Do you know what Stark is saying about you?"

"I can only imagine," said Minis, forcing a smile. "And I also imagine the spirits are doing all the talking. It's nothing but the ranting of a sore loser."

July 1832, The Owens House

Parties at the Owens House always made Stark feel like royalty. It didn't matter to him that it wasn't his house, his hooch or his smokes. After a couple of belts of the good stuff and a puff or two on a big ol' stogie, Stark was living the high life.

A slender servant worked her way through the crowd. In her arms, she carried a handcrafted cedar box. Stark waved her over. She bowed her head, and then curtsied. Stark cradled her chin in his hand, encouraging her to look up at him. Instead, she shyly turned her gaze away and opened the box for him. Stark smiled and hastily selected a fat candela. He nodded his thanks as she walked away.

Stark bit off the end of his cigar and looked around for a suitable place to spit. Finding none, he waded through the tightly packed parlor to the main entrance. He opened the heavy wooden doors, leaned out and spit the soggy tobacco over the railing. Then, he lifted the glass globe from the hurricane lantern near the door and lit the torpedo with a few quick puffs.

He stepped out onto the portico. Though the night air was sultry, it was a refreshing change from the stuffy atmosphere in the parlor. As Stark pulled the door closed, he felt it tugged from his grip. He turned around to see Dr. Arnold.

"Mr. Stark," said the doctor, packing his pipe. "Mind if I join you?"

Stark puffed on his cigar.

"Beautiful night," said Arnold, "Can you imagine, the Marquis de Lafayette stood on this very spot, not ten years ago?"

"It wasn't here," said Stark, frustrated by the fraying edge of an otherwise fine cigar. "It was from the side gallery."

"Still...."

Dr. Arnold leaned against the rail and struck a small wooden match on the underside of the balustrade. It sparked and sputtered to life. Stark leaned away from the pyrotechnic display.

"Fascinating things, these matches," said Arnold, firing up his pipe. "A friend of mine brought them from Germany. They only work about half the time, and I've already burned my fingers a time or two, but there's something to be said for the convenience."

Stark gazed at the starlit sky. Arnold regarded him coolly, and then turned his gaze skyward.

"This business between you and Dr. Minis," said Dr. Arnold. "Did you ever apologize for the remark you made back at Luddington's?"

"Why would I want to do that?" said Stark leaning hard on the rail. He was now chewing on his stogie more than he was puffing. The torpedo had burned out shortly after Arnold lit his pipe. "Apologizin' ain't gonna change my opinion of the man."

"But certainly you'd agree that such scurrilous speech would call into question a man's honor," said Arnold.

"Yes, sir," said Stark, eyeing Arnold. "Provided he had any honor to begin with. Know what else?"

Arnold raised his eyebrows.

"He ain't worth the powder and shot it would take to kill him."

July 1832, Coits Club, on the Outskirts of Savannah

The iron ring bounced once in the sand and then rested on the metal stake. A second ring followed in short order. This time, the inside lip caught the stake and the ring wobbled downward, to a comfortable rest on the first.

Dr. Minis dusted his hands while Dr. Arnold and Charles Spalding applauded.

"Well, Philip," said Dr. Arnold, "I dare say you have the steadiest hands in all of Savannah."

"It's not over yet," said Spalding. He held up a metal ring and eyed the stake, several paces away.

"Come now, Mr. Spalding. You'd have to get three ringers in a row just to tie the good doctor," said Arnold.

Spalding ceased the swaying movement of his arm to glare at Dr. Arnold. Arnold replied by holding his hands up in a gesture of mock-defense. As Spalding resumed the warm up to his pitch, Arnold blustered a cough. Minis tried to conceal his grin with a forced, thoughtful expression. Spalding found himself grinning as he launched the ring.

It hooked, and bounced into the grass.

"The hell with it," said Spalding. "Good show, gents. Well played."

The men gathered their belongings and walked to the carriage. Dr. Arnold held the coat for Dr. Minis as he rolled down his sleeves.

"I saw our good friend, Stark, last night," said Arnold.

"At the party at the Owens House?"

"Yes," said Arnold. "He's still pretty upset over his loss."

"Come now," said Minis, tugging sharply on his crisp sleeve. "I find that hard to believe."

"Well, I believe it to be true," said Arnold. "Especially since he has still offered no apology for slandering your good name."

"Richard," said Dr. Minis, fastening his cuffs. "I do believe I told you that his words were induced by a night of hard drinking and a stiff, red neck."

"Perhaps," said Dr. Arnold, offering the coat for Dr. Minis. "But if a man were to insult not only my good name, but the reputation of my ancestors, and of my race...."

"I've let this go," said Dr. Minis, shrugging into his coat. "Perhaps you should, too."

"Philip," said the doctor, holding the door to the carriage. "You should at least demand an apology, if not satisfaction. Word is spreading that you are a man without honor — and a coward. I should think you would have a vested interest in such an affair."

Dr. Minis stepped onto the runner of the carriage, but stopped for a moment to address his friend and colleague.

"Dr. Arnold, I shall request from Mr. Stark that satisfaction which one gentleman should afford another." He looked to Charles Spalding.

"And I would ask that you, Mr. Spalding, my dear friend, deliver it on my behalf." He turned his gaze back to Dr. Arnold.

"But, honestly, Richard, this is, to quote the Great Bard, 'much ado about nothing'."

August 9, 1832, the Offices of Dr. Philip Minis

A knock at the door called Dr. Minis away from his writing. He sprinkled a little desiccant onto the pages of his ledger, and closed the heavy book.

"Come."

Dr. Minis looked up as Charles Spalding entered the room. He rose to greet his old friend.

"Charles, what a pleasant surprise!" The doctor extended a hand across the desk. After a quick handshake, Charles reached in his breast pocket and pulled a sealed letter.

"What is this?" asked Dr. Minis.

"Mr. Stark responded to your request." Dr. Minis took the letter from Mr. Spalding. He opened the drawer to his desk, removed a silver letter opener, and used it to break the seal. Minis chuckled.

"Sir?"

"Is he serious?" asked the doctor, easing into his high-backed chair.

"Quite serious," said Mr. Spalding.

"Rifles? Today at 5?" Dr. Minis looked over his reading glasses at the grandfather clock.

"Yes," said Spalding, checking his pocket watch against the clock. "And it's already noon."

"Such an awkward weapon for a duel, I should think." Minis pulled a sheet of parchment from his desk drawer and laid it upon the felt. He removed the cap from his inkwell and dipped his tortoiseshell pen into the ink.

"Give this to Mr. Wayne. He is Mr. Stark's second, is he not?"

"He is, sir."

Minis pinched a little sodium calcium powder and sprinkled it onto the parchment. He turned in his chair and carefully blew the desiccant across the page. He leaned over his desk and folded the paper. The doctor reached in his desk drawer, removed a wax stick and waved it over the flickering flame of his desk lamp until it was just starting to melt. He carefully pressed it onto the folded parchment, and sealed it by pressing the wax with a brass stamp. Then he rose and handed the letter to Mr. Spalding.

August 9, 1832, the Residence of Thomas M. Wayne

"I don't care that his rifle is at the gunsmiths," said Mr. Wayne. "According to the Code Duello, Dr. Minis must abide by the time and place set by the challenged, in this case, Mr. Stark."

"The code also states, quite clearly, that the challenger has first right of refusal." Mr. Spalding turned for the door. As he reached the door handle, he said, "Any time tomorrow is suitable for myself and for Dr. Minis."

August 9, 1832, Screven's Ferry, South Carolina

Stark and Wayne trudged up the short hill to the bluff overlooking the Back River. Over the scattered trees on Hutchinson Island, they could make out the Savannah skyline. Though it was just after five, the sun had hours to go before setting.

"Did you tell Dr. Minis that I had an extra rifle for him?" said Stark. He funneled gunpowder down the rifle's barrel.

"It wasn't in my instructions to do so," said Wayne, handing Stark a musket ball. "But he did say he'd meet us tomorrow."

"And tomorrow, and tomorrow, and tomorrow...." Stark drove the musket ball home with a quick thrust of the ramrod.

The men nodded. Stark brought his rifle to bear on the absent Dr. Minis, and fired a volley into thin air. Then, he cradled the rifled and looked to his friend.

"Shall we?"

August 9, 1832, Burrough's Counting Room

Dr. Minis and Mr. Cohen stepped onto Bull Street.

"Do you really think they went to Screvens Ferry?" asked Cohen.

"Why should I care?" said Minis. "I responded to his articles in good faith. I trust he'll respond in kind."

"Perhaps you give him too much credit, my friend."

As the men wandered through Johnson Square discussing the day's events, they heard Dr. Arnold's voice call from East Bryan Street.

"Gentlemen! Shall we put away the day with a pint at the City Hotel?"

The men all shook hands.

"It has been a rather long day," said Dr. Minis. "I suppose one pint wouldn't do any harm."

"I'd been meaning to go there, anyway," said Mr. Cohen. "My wife keeps talking about Mr. Audubon's new book. She says I simply must acquire a copy for her."

"Fancies birds, does she?" asked Dr. Arnold.

"Yes," said Cohen. "And since Mr. Audubon is staying at the hotel...."

"I hear he is autographing copies," said Dr. Minis.

As they rounded the corner onto Bay Street, Minis nearly ran headlong into Stark. Cohen and Arnold exchanged nervous glances as Stark glared hard at coolly composed Minis. Wayne hustled over just as Stark reached for the blade tucked in his belt. He placed firm hands on Stark's arms and guided him away from the men.

Minis, Cohen, and Arnold watched as Wayne rushed Stark down Bull Street; his angry words lingered in Johnson Square.

"Let me go back and whip the damned rascal!"

Dr. Minis removed his top hat and smoothed his hair with a steady hand.

"Gentlemen?"

As they resumed their walk down Bay Street, toward the City Hotel, Dr. Arnold leaned into Dr. Minis.

"Philip, I feel that you should not act solely on the defensive. I fear for your reputation, and for your very life!"

"Tomorrow, Richard," said Minis. "It all ends tomorrow."

August 10, 1832, City Hotel

The City Hotel had a reputation as a rough-and-tumble place. From the soldier to the scallywag, young men — all with something to prove — seemed to gravitate to the bar of the City Hotel; and more than one "sporting debate" ended with pistols-at-paces, the duels taking place on the other side of the Savannah River. Therefore, it was no accident that Dr. Minis chose to meet Stark in the barroom of the hotel. Still, the weight of the pistol was of little comfort to Minis.

"Easy now," he thought. *We're just having words.*

Mr. Spalding held the door for Minis. As he entered the lobby, Minis unbuttoned his coat to allow for a quick draw, should his last attempt at diplomacy fail.

"Phillip...." Spalding grabbed Minis by the arm. Minis turned and glared at his second. Spalding relaxed his grip, but kept his steely gaze focused on the doctor.

"It has to be this way, Charles," said Minis, staring off into space. He jerked his arm out of Spalding's hand. "I'm tired of running."

"Shall I meet you in the bar?" said Spalding. Minis turned on his heel and, with a dismissive wave, stalked toward the stairs.

Spalding watched as Dr. Minis moved through the lobby. He threw a shilling or two at the paperboy, and busied himself with a quick browse through the paper. Barely a page into his reading, Spalding saw Minis stride around the corner.

"Mr. Mann informs me that Mr. Stark and Mr. Wayne are upstairs."

"Are we meeting them there, then?"

"No," said Minis. "I've asked him to invite them downstairs to join us for a drink."

The men strode through the main room and settled in the bar. Minis barely noticed the crowd of men and women gathered in the lobby, and it was just as well. He had to stay focused. He was taking a chance in calling Stark out in a public place; given the man's tendencies toward belligerence, one misstep would certainly end in tragedy. Still, Minis felt this was a calculated risk. At least he would be on record, in the public's mind, anyway, as a man who is willing to defend his honor.

Several minutes passed. Spalding thrust his nose back in the evening paper. Minis kept a wayward eye on the door, and one hand resting comfortably on the caplock. Just when Minis was about to check in again with the concierge, he heard Stark and Wayne coming down the stairs. Stark was hard to ignore, as he was already bragging about how he would beat some sense into Minis once he laid eyes on him.

Minis stepped through the door and turned. Before Stark could reach the last step, he declared in a voice loud enough for all in the room to hear, "I pronounce thee, James Jones Stark, a coward!"

Stark reached in his coat and rushed toward Minis. Minis, in one smooth motion, drew his pistol, cocked the hammer, and fired. Stark was practically on top of Minis when the cap finally ignited the powder. The bullet ripped through his chest and shot across the room, slamming into the kitchen door.

The report from the pistol rattled drinking glasses. Men and women scrambled to safety, some stumbling onto Bay Street. Spalding tossed his paper in the air and fought the panicked crowd. By the time he reached Minis, Wayne was trying to wrest the pistol from the grip of the doctor.

Doctors Waring and Arnold had heard the pandemonium from the mayor's office across the street. They rushed over to the City Hotel. Earlier in the day, Dr. Waring urged members of the Anti-dueling Association to mediate this growing dispute between Stark and Minis, and now Dr. Waring knew they were too late.

Dr. Arnold shoved his way through the gawking onlookers. There, slumped on the floor, was James Jones Stark. The doctor quickly examined Stark's gaping wound, and checked the man's pulse.

"He's dead," said the doctor.

He looked up at his friend, Dr. Minis. Disheveled and crazed, Minis struggled against Wayne and Spalding. At one point, the doctor threatened to fire into the crowd, somehow forgetting that he had yet to reload.

"My carriage is across Bay at the Exchange," said Dr. Arnold. "Tell the driver to take him to my office. I'll have the sheriff meet us there...."

January 1833

The bailiff peered into the room and motioned toward counsel.

"Well, gentlemen," said Mr. Charlton, pocketing his watch. "It appears the jury has made up their minds."

The defense team settled into the courtroom and waited for the arrival of Judge Dougherty. Dr. Minis leaned over to Mr. Charlton.

"I thought a short deliberation was only good news for the prosecution," he whispered.

"We shall see."

The bailiff held the chambers door for Judge Dougherty. His arrival prompted those gathered in the courtroom to rise to their feet in anticipation of the bailiff's request.

"All rise! Chatham County Court is now in session. The honorable Charles Dougherty presiding."

The judge smoothed his robes and settled into his chair.

"Please be seated," said the judge, sifting through various documents.

"I understand you have reached a verdict. Will you please hand the bailiff your decision?"

The foreman stood and handed a slip of paper to the bailiff, who brought it over to Judge Dougherty. The judge unfolded the parchment and read the decision to himself. He jotted down a few notes, and then looked to the jury.

"Please read your decision to the court, Mr. Foreman."

"In the matter of the State vs. Dr. Philip Minis, on the charge of murder, we, the jury, find the defendant...."

Minis bowed his head, and drew in a deep breath. He was prepared for the worst.

"Not guilty."

Dr. Minis slumped into his chair. It was finally over.

No one knows what Stark was reaching for on that August day. No weapon was found on his person. The Anti-dueling Association did send letters encouraging arbitration; though Mr. Spalding never received his letter before he and Dr. Minis left for the City Hotel. James Stark did receive his, and was considering his reply when he decided to go to the City Hotel. After his acquittal, Dr. Minis would go on to serve his country as a surgeon in the U.S. Army, would father seven children, and would serve on several benevolent committees here in Savannah. Despite growing opposition to "affairs of honor" and the link to intemperance, dueling would continue in Savannah until 1877, when two lawyers met to argue not with words in court, but with pistols at dusk. Both survived, having missed their marks, and went on to be successful leaders.

This story originally appeared in Savannah Ghosts: Haunts of the Hostess City – Tales that Still Spook Savannah.

Boilermaker

1 oz. Blended whiskey
12 oz. Beer

Fill a shot glass with whiskey. Pour the beer into a beer mug. Shoot the whiskey. Sip the beer. NEVER drop the shot glass into the beer, unless you relish broken teeth.

On shot glasses: If your barkeep only fills the shot to the line screened onto the glass, you're only getting half a shot. In a 2-ounce shot glass, that line marks 1 ounce. Traditionally, a good barkeep will pour the liquor until there is surface tension.

On whiskey: "Whiskey" comes from the Gaelic word, "uisgebaugh," and means, "water of life." When pronounced it correctly, it sounds something like WIS-GER-BAW. Their British cousins couldn't quite wrap their stiff upper lips around the word and pronounced it "whiskey."

Come to Scratch

David Harland Rousseau

December 1864

Every time Red Pickrin passed the Mercer House, he wanted to spit. The house promised to be a real jewel in Savannah's crown, and he was proud to have had a hand in building it. But the cold shadow of civil war blanketed the land, taking with it the best and brightest, among them, General Hugh Mercer. While the good General was off fighting for Southern honor and states' rights, his brick Italianate home would remain unfinished and boarded up — along with any hope of Red finishing his apprenticeship as a mason.

Five years, he thought. *Five damn long years.*

When the call to arms went out to all able-bodied Southern men, Red was among the first to stand in the back of the line. Oh, he wanted to fight, all right, but Red always had a way of showing up a little too late. It was his nature. He would have lost the bricklaying job at the Mercer house if a friend of a friend hadn't talked his dear sweet mother into snatchin' him up by the ear and draggin' him to the work site at Monterey Square, just north of Forsyth Park. (Some might have said that Red was a bit of a mama's boy — except for his mama, that is.)

Still, Red made his way to the recruiting station and found the square mobbed with recruits, young and old — all eager to live and die for Dixie. By the time he got anywhere near the front of the line, they were turning folks away. Still, Red made a point of talking loud to the sergeant — if for no other reason than to show those around him that he gave a damn. The sergeant politely took his information and promised to contact him should the need arise.

Sometime during 1862, Mrs. Pickrin heard a knock at the door. A Confederate sergeant came a-callin' for young Red and said the Confederacy was in dire need of his services. Having lost a husband and her oldest son to the Dreadful Pestilence some eight years earlier, she wasn't about to lose her youngest due to the Recent Unpleasantness. Oh no. That would never do. So, while Red was out taking up odd jobs and lending a hand where he could, she feigned an illness, or two. She swore she was suffering from a relapse of Yellow Fever (until Red found the emetics under her bed). Then, she claimed she had a wasting disease (until the physician said she was healthy as a horse, which Mrs. Pickrin took as an insult to her "womanly figure" and took to beating the doctor about the head and shoulders). In the end, Red decided that it was best for him to stay home and care for his mama, lest she die of a broken heart.

Now, having seen what the Union had done to his beloved Savannah, he'd've given his right arm for the chance to shoot a couple of Yanks. Like a plague of locusts, they descended upon his city, tearing up everything in their path. By some accounts, Sherman's men had already removed a couple of thousand cartloads of manure — and they still had a ways to go. (Some, like Mrs. Pickrin, thought that the Union soldiers themselves ought to be piled high on those carts of manure as they were wheeled out of the city proper.)

And so, as was his habit, Red trudged by the Mercer House and found a whole new reason to spit fire: those damned Yanks were tearing the boards off the windows and were using them to construct lean-tos against the Pulaski Monument!

"Hell, no!" spat Red, rolling up his sleeves. He looked for the man with the most stripes on his sleeve and trudged on over, ready to take on the whole damned Union Army, if he had to.

Private Beechnut hadn't been in the Union Army for much longer than the time it had taken him to march through boot camp. The way he saw it, a stint in the military was a good way to get out of being an ironworker. Better still, it was a great way to get out of Cleveland. Now here he was, serving in the Union Army under that great general, William Tecumseh Sherman — and at the end of his March to the Sea at that. Beechnut had hoped to record all that he had seen, but the army never saw fit to teach him to read or write. So, he stumbled along, asking others to write his letters for him. It was a leap of faith, since he still had a very limited understanding of the written word. For all he knew, his "buddies" could have been telling tall tales about his exploits. (In a way, he kind of hoped they would. After all, Beechnut had a girl to impress back home. No, they weren't engaged, nor were they even courting, but he wanted to impress her just the same.)

Beechnut and his bunkmate, Corporal Newbury, wedged their bayonets into the space between the brick and the boards and wrenched the planks off the windows.

"I hear this is the home of a Confederate General!" said Beechnut.

"Yep," said Newbury. "Hugh Mercer. Don't know much about him, though."

"Me, neither," said Beechnut. "But I still don't get why we can't all just bunk in the house itself."

"Unit cohesiveness," said Newbury.

"Unit what?" The men cradled the planks under their arms and stepped back from the house.

"It means we all live under the same rules and conditions." An ammunition caisson rumbled by. Newbury raised a free hand to wave at the riders as they passed.

"It wouldn't do if we were all cozy in this brick home while our comrades at arms slept under the stars, now would it?"

"Guess not," said Beechnut.

"Besides," said Newbury, "we'll need the wood floors for firewood."

Suddenly, Beechnut crashed into the back of Newbury.

"Dammit, Beechnut!"

"It wasn't me!" said Beechnut. "I was shoved!"

The two men looked over their shoulders to find Red Pickrin, mad as a Kentucky gamecock.

Beechnut sprang to his feet and shoved Pickrin hard. Pickrin stumbled back.

"What the hell do you think you're doing, cracker!"

Pickrin stood nose to nose with Beechnut. "Y'all ain't got no business tearin' up this house! Now take these boards an' put 'em back where you found 'em!"

Newbury placed a firm hand on Beechnut's shoulder. Beechnut backed away from the men.

"You know we can't do that, sir," said Newbury. His was a smile that seemed warm at first blush, but left a man cold. "We need to make camp."

"I could give a rat's ass," Red snarled. "Y'all come wanderin' into town like you own the place — which you don't — and y'all promised to take care of our people and our property — which you ain't — "

Newbury flashed that unnerving smile like he was running for office. "Sir, I understand your — "

"You understand nothin'." Red punctuated his remark with a hock and spit. He looked around and found a crowd of bluecoats gathering, every one of them a little more than eager to beat the tar out of the hotheaded Johnny Reb.

"Look around you, son," said the corporal, his smile fading into an icy, clenched-jaw stare. "You can't win this fight."

"Not today," said Red. He shoved his way past Newbury and Beechnut.

Red stomped up the stairs of their modest townhouse at Mary Marshall Row. He fumbled with the keys, stepped in, and slammed the door.

"Red Pickrin!" came the sound of his mother's voice. "You know better than to slam the door when you walk in!"

Red said nothing. He knew anything out of his mouth would set her off even more, and apologizing for something he felt justified in doing, well, that wasn't about to happen. Instead, he quietly blew out a breath and made his way upstairs to the master bedroom. About half way up, he heard his mother call again.

"Red, baby."

Her voice just gets on my nerves.

"Bring Mama some sweet tea before you come up."

Red sighed and walked back downstairs, hoping to find some already made up. When he got to the pantry, he cursed.

Of course, there ain't no sweet tea.

He opened a canister, then another, and another.

Ain't got no tea. No sugar. That's just great.

He plodded to the bottom of the stairs, leaned on the banister and called up to his mother.

"Mama," he called. "Ain't no sweet tea."

"What?!?"

Red took a breath. He just knew what was coming.

"Ain't got no sweet tea, Mama."

Mrs. Pickrin shifted her great weight in her bed. She heard Red quite clearly — she had excellent hearing — but hated being barked at. She did, after all, carry the little whelp in her belly for nearly a year.

"Baby, you know I can't hear all that well. Not since the fever." She stretched out her thick arm and gazed at her tiny little nails, as if they were diamonds in the rough. "Now come on up and talk to me like a gentleman."

Red trudged up the stairs. Slowly, he rounded the banister. Then, he shuffled to the door of his mother's room. He leaned in the doorway and dropped his head.

"Ain't no sweet tea, Mama."

"No sweet tea? Go make your mama some sweet tea, baby."

"Can't, Mama." Red stared at the wall.

Mrs. Pickrin supported herself on her elbows.

"Well, why not?" Mrs. Pickrin had a way of finishing most of her sentences with jaw-agape. Sometimes, depending on the inflection, her jowls would wobble for about a second after she pronounced the last syllable.

"We got no sugar. No tea. Can't make your sweet tea without them, now can I?" Oh, he was fighting hard to be civil.

"Did you have a bad day baby? Just go on down to market an' get what we need."

"Can't."

"Now you're jus' bein' difficult."

"Mama," he could feel his temples throb. "Maybe it's been a while since you went to market yourself — and I know you're not feeling well — but things are… different."

Mrs. Pickrin shoved herself upright.

"In my drawer is some money — "

Red ripped open the drawer and seized a handful of Confederate dollars.

"This money?" He slammed the drawer shut.

"This?!" Red stalked over to the bed and fluttered the bills in her face. Mrs. Pickrin grabbed the covers and drew them up to hide.

"This money was worthless — WORTHLESS — before them Yanks rolled into town. How much do you think it is worth now? Hmmm?! *Before* they showed up, you'd have to tote a lifesavings in a market basket. You know what that got you, Mama? A half-a-sack of grits — maybe! And then, you'd have to leave the basket as payment!

"Now we need greenbacks — and lots of them — and we ain't got no way to get 'em!"

Mrs. Pickrin tried hard to still her quivering lip. Red stomped over to the dresser and yarded open drawer after drawer.

"Any greenbacks hiding in here? No. Of course not! Because you never leave this room!"

Red heard a soft sniffle come from under the covers. He dropped his head and quietly closed the last drawer.

"I'm sorry, Mama." He couldn't bear to look at her. He knew he wouldn't be able to say what he wanted to say if he did. Instead, he traced small circles in the dust on the dresser.

"It's just that, well, I missed my chance... and now, it's too late to do anything about it."

Red turned toward the door. He knew he should rush right over and comfort his mother, but he just couldn't break through that wall that had been building inside him ever since the recruiting sergeant turned him away. He always wondered why he was never called to service....

"I'll get your sweet tea, Mama." Red shuffled out the door. As he started down the stairs, he whispered, "Somehow."

He knew that getting tea, let alone sugar, would be a Sisyphean task. The Yanks were the only ones in town with any money to spend — and none of it went back to rebuilding the crippled economy. Sure, Billy Yank was all too happy to throw money after lame horses on some makeshift racetrack. He was even happier to take advantage of starving Confederate widows, assuaging his guilt by leaving a few greenbacks on her bedside table. Then, as he threw more money at the bartenders, he would sully her good name by bragging about his conquest.

Red glanced up to see a couple of young ladies cross the street expressly to avoid walking under the Union flag. How he admired their courage. Even in their threadbare dresses, these ladies carried themselves with both prevenient grace and steel-jawed courage. Such resolve prompted Sherman himself to say that Savannah women were "the toughest set" he ever knew. One moment, the Confederate wives were selling sweetbread to the bluecoats, and the next, these same women would turn their backs on those same soldiers as they passed in muster.

Sherman was right, he thought. *The women of Savannah would have kept this war going long after the men had given up.*

Red crossed Drayton Street at Bay Lane. He knew the barkeep, Johnny Ray, and hoped that he might know of anyone who was hiring. As he opened the door, Newbury and Beechnut staggered out. He thought about jumping them in the lane, but knew that would be suicide.

Keep it holstered, he told himself. Red breathed a sigh of relief when the men passed without recognizing him. Oh, he was ready to throw down, all right, but now wasn't the time or the place.

He stepped into the room. The place was crawling with bluecoats, two or three deep at the bar. He shook his head. He'd never get Johnny Ray's attention at this rate, and he just couldn't bear the thought of jumping behind the bar to serve these sons-a-bitches, even if it meant sweet tea for his mama. But as Red turned to leave, a broadsheet tacked to the doorpost caught his eye. The header read: *Last Man Standing*. Red snatched the sheet off the wall and bolted out the door. He found himself a way to get some money — and beat some Yankee ass!

Red loved to scrap. Granted, sometimes it was in the defense of his mother's good name (often due to his mother's public preening and doting), but Red had to thank his mama, even for that. He knew that he could hold his own if it came to blows, and he was glad. It would soon pay off, hopefully big!

The Yanks, in their boredom, started holding boxing matches in the backrooms of barrooms, especially behind the pub where Johnny Ray worked. Granted, you had to enter from the alley, but that worked just fine. Those that wanted to bet on the fight could; those that just wanted to put away the day wouldn't be bothered by the rowdy crowd.

Johnny Ray was a sharp guy. He took on the responsibility of taking bets, keeping the odds, posting the rankings, and he did a fine job of it — especially for a man who had to learn it all on the fly. That Johnny Ray was the one pairing up the fighters was good news for Red. If all went according to his plan (and if Johnny Ray agreed), Red would only have to fight Yankees, and he had one in mind — that private he saw ripping boards off the Mercer House. There was no rhyme or reason for his hatred of the young man. After all, they were about the same age and might have even been good friends in nobler times, but like two dogs who can't stand each other's scent, he just wanted to tear into that kid like nobody's business.

Red waited around until Johnny Ray was closing up, and then invited himself in for a drink. Johnny Ray listened to Red's plan, and waited until he said what he had to say.

"Sorry, Red," said Johnny Ray. "It doesn't work that way."

"Why the hell not?"

Johnny Ray leaned on the bar. "Because the Yanks have this bruiser that's been bustin' jaws all week. Some ringer they brought in from Massachusetts. I hear he's down here, settin' things up for a colored regiment."

"Is he a Negro?"

"Naw, man. Some mick from Beantown. He'll clean your clock, son. I seen it."

"Then put me in first, so I can get it over with."

Not long after donning the gray, Johnny Ray Banks found himself on the mist-shrouded battlefield of Chickamauga Creek. Shrapnel from an exploding mortar took his left eye and shattered his eardrum. The blast knocked him so cold that, in the fog of war, his comrades had all but left him for dead. Needless to say, Johnny never talked much about the war, and folks knew better than to ask. In a strange way, the bluecoats that now frequented his pub did so because they wanted to lay eyes on a gray-back who survived that bloody battle. Johnny Ray didn't care, as long as they kept tipping.

Yep, Johnny Ray had seen a lot of things in his thirty-five years, so when he looked into Red's eyes, he witnessed the fire of a young man who had already forged his decision.

"You're in," said Johnny Ray. And with that, he scratched the name of some Yankee private named Beechnut off the list, and wrote: *R. Pickrin*.

Friday night came fast. Red made up some excuse about picking up a last minute delivery job for Johnny Ray. He certainly didn't want his mother to know about his plan for winning five hundred greenbacks — the prize for defeating the Yankee Bruiser, as he was now called. She would worry herself sick.

Despite the curfew, the back room to the pub was packed with rowdies and regulars. A handful of carpetbaggers intending to pass through Savannah on the way to Charleston found themselves with little to do, since so many pubs and restaurants had closed up earlier than expected. They placed the highest bets of all — and always on the odds-on favorite.

"Gentlemen, please!" said Johnny Ray, holding up his hands. "Y'all just settle down, now."

A hush fell over the room.

"Alright, then. If you hadn't placed your bet on the first fight, you flat outta luck. Time has done run out."

A murmur rolled through the room as bluecoats clutched their tickets.

"Now, our champ-een has been cleaning the clocks of young bucks all week."

The crowd stomped their feet and cheered. Johnny Ray held his hands up, waving them down a bit.

"Hopefully tonight, he won't be quite so bored."

Bluecoats guffawed and snickered.

"This is a *Last Man Standing* bout," said Johnny Ray, thrusting a finger at the elimination brackets tacked to the wall. "Y'all know what that means. The longer our champ stays in the ring, the larger the pot grows."

The men hooted and cheered.

"If he becomes the last man standing, he stands to win half of the prize money — which I suspect will go a long way to nurse his wounds!"

A raucous laughter filled the room. With a gleam in his eye, Johnny Ray continued.

"I know it's unlikely, but if a challenger should best our champ — "

The men in blue booed and jeered. Johnny Ray raised his voice to shout above the noise.

"If a challenger should defeat our champ, he'll take home five-hundred greenbacks and come on back next week to become the Last Man Standing!"

The Yanks stomped their feet and threw playful jabs at each other. Johnny kept right on talking.

"Now, if you still don't know about Broughton's Rules, I ain't gonna explain 'em now, except to say that the round doesn't end until one of 'em gets knocked on his ass, and the fight doesn't end until one of 'em is slapped so silly he can't come to scratch. Could take five minutes. Could last all night.

"So, without further delay, let me call these boys in here."

Private Beechnut slid out of his jacket and was already receiving pats on the back from Newbury and the boys.

"Our first fighter is a local boy, from right here in Savannah."

Beechnut and Newbury exchanged awkward glances.

"Weighing in at a very lean 170 pounds, R-r-r-r-ed Pickrin-n-n-n-n!"

As the crowd jeered, Red bounced his way passed the stunned Beechnut and Newbury. He stepped in the ring and gave a quick nod and a wink to Beechnut. He then thumped his chest with his fists and pointed at Newbury. Johnny Ray glanced around and waited for the crowd to settle. With a flourish, he raised his hands high.

"And now, all the way from Boston, Massachusetts...."

The room exploded with stomping feet and warlike cries.

"Tipping the scales at a whopping 210 pounds...."

The Bruiser shrugged out of his jacket — and he had to work at it. Johnny Ray motioned toward the big Irishman.

"The Yankee-e-e-e Bruiser-r-r...."

The big Irishman threw a couple of lighting fast jabs to the delight of the crowd and danced into the makeshift ring.

"Kerr-r-r-r-y Garr-r-r-rett!!!!"

The thunderous applause erupting from the Yanks never bothered Red, nor did it bother him that the Bruiser was a head taller. Red had all the focus and tenacity of a foxhound on a rabbit. The intensity of his stare and the wild look in his eyes made the Bruiser shift his gaze, if only for a split second.

"If you're gonna fight under my roof," said Johnny Ray, "then you're gonna fight by the rules. Don't hit a man when he's down. Don't wrestle or tackle. Don't fight like a girl and pull hair or nothin'. Round ends when one a'y'all takes a knee or gets knocked down, and if ya can't come to this line right here after half-a-minute, that's all she wrote. Got it?"

The men nodded. Red spit on the floor.

"Now, I'm gonna get on out the way," Johnny Ray said. "When I do, y'all start fightin'."

Before Johnny Ray could slip out of the makeshift ring, Red threw a vicious right cross, knocking the Bruiser to the floor. The men jeered and cussed.

"Get up!" said the prancing Red. "I'm'o whoop yer ass, boy!"

The Bruiser brushed his lip with the back of his hand. Red clenched his fists. He had waited for this moment for too long. Four years of pulling his punches and holding his tongue, all for the sake of Southern decorum and mother's modesty, was directed at the burly brute that, in Red's mind, had become the very symbol of Northern Oppression. Someone was going to fall tonight, and Red was going to make damn sure it wasn't him.

"Get up!"

The Bruiser stood and brought his fists up. He stepped for the line. The moment he came to scratch, Red threw the same right cross. The Bruiser ducked and smashed Red in the gut. He doubled over. The Yank followed with a brutal uppercut, sending Red into the crowd. The bluecoats shoved Red back at the Bruiser, who launched a heavy-handed cross. Red bobbed and landed a sharp hook to the Yank's ribs. The Bruiser wheeled around and clumsily threw a left. Red ducked and popped him in the ribs again, then threw a right hook at the Yank's head. Their arms locked, and the men found themselves in a tight clinch.

"Not bad, kid," the Bruiser growled. "You got a lot of heart!"

Red shoved the Bruiser off, sending him into the crowd. A couple of men shoved the Bruiser headlong into Red's waiting fists.

Men booed.

Bruiser stumbled back. The gavel fell.

CLACK-CLACK

"I'm alright," said the Bruiser, bouncing to his feet. He glided into the ring, threw a jab, then another, then a quick shot to the gut, followed by a sharp hook to Red's head. Red crumpled to the floor.

Men cheered.

"Kick his cracker ass!"

The gavel fell. Newbury slapped Beechnut across the back and shouted.

"I told you this was gonna be good!"

And so it went, the boxer versus the brawler. Some rounds lasted a few seconds. Some lasted more than twenty minutes.

Worn and weary, his eye cut and swollen, the Bruiser stumbled into Red who threw a sharp jab at the Bruiser's wounded eye. The Bruiser stumbled back, but was pursued relentlessly by Red, who pummeled him, one sharp, hard blow after another.

The Bruiser collapsed at Newbury's feet. The corporal took a knee and tried to rouse the big Yank.

"Kerry!" said Newbury. "Get up, you chicken-shit Mick!"

Johnny Ray banged the gavel.

CLACK-CLACK-CLACK

Newbury turned ashen. Murmurs echoed throughout the room. Bluecoats cussed and tore up their tickets. Locals laughed. Red staggered a bit, and then dragged a sweaty forearm across his bloody mouth.

"He killed him!" shouted Newbury. He sprang to his feet and thrust a finger at the now-sluggish Red. "That cracker killed him!"

Union troops pounced on Red like a pack of rabid dogs. Too weak to fight back, all he could do was take the beating: hard kicks to the ribs, sharp punches to the face and head. Red found himself smiling. He couldn't help himself. He just knew that sweet tea would taste so good.

"That son of a bitch!" cried a stocky sergeant. "I'll take that smile right off his face!"

The soldier raised his leg high and drove the arch of his riding boot onto Red's neck.

CRACK!

An eerie hush fell over the room. The men looked at one another with fear in their eyes. Before anyone knew what had really happened, they heard a quiet murmur from the corner of the room. The Bruiser stirred and groaned.

The Yanks exchanged nervous glances as Johnny Ray forced his way through the crowd.

Johnny felt a wave of nausea roll over him when he saw Red's lifeless body. He slumped to the floor and gathered Red in his arms. He watched helplessly as Red's head lolled to one side, like that of a rag doll. Then, with a soldier's resolve, Johnny Ray Banks carefully laid Red down and draped the young man's coat over his battered face. He dropped his head just long enough to catch his breath.

"Who did this?" Johnny asked. He scanned the room. Carpetbaggers were slinking out the back as if nothing had happened. Johnny looked up to see Corporal Newbury patting a sergeant on the shoulder.

"Got somethin' to tell me, corporal?" he said. He seized Newbury's arm and wheeled him around. Johnny Ray was met with that blasted smile.

"Your friend put up one hell of a fight," said Newbury. "Surprised us all."

"You kill him?" Johnny Ray stood nose-to-nose with Newbury. "Or was it that ape of a sergeant?"

Without flinching, Newbury called out.

"Sergeant Grimes. Did you break this man's neck?"

Grimes folded his arms.

"He died in the fight, corporal," sneered Grimes.

Newbury smirked.

"Private Beechnut."

The young private straightened up.

"Yes, sir?"

"Who killed this man?"

Beechnut lowered his eyes. He found himself suddenly pre-occupied by the leather band of his kepi.

"I can't hear you, private!"

Beechnut snapped up.

"He died in the fight, corporal!"

Newbury smiled. How he loved unit cohesion.

"I may be wrong, Mr. Banks, but if I took roll right here and now, I bet I'd find a room full of Union soldiers who would all say that your friend here died in the fight."

He inched closer to Johnny Ray.

"So, tell me, Mr. Banks," said Newbury, as the bluecoats closed ranks. "Do you think a one-eyed Jack can beat a full house?"

Days had passed, and Mrs. Pickrin still heard no word from her son. Given that Red was the only one to check in on her, Mrs. Pickrin took it upon herself to dress, but one look at the moth-eaten garment and she realized that she could no longer fit into it. She waddled over to a steamer trunk, pulled out some black fabric and her sewing kit, and began stitching herself a new dress. It took her a week of hand stitching to finish the dress, and she found herself marveling at the delicate work.

How long has it been? She wondered.

She bathed herself, stepped into her dress, and looked for her shoes. From under the bed, she dragged a pair of dust-covered, ankle-high boots. She braced her great weight on the bed and forced herself up with a grunt. Then, she eased herself onto the worn bed. With a grumble, she dragged her ankle up onto her knee and tried to shoehorn her wide foot into the boot. Now two sizes too small, she knew they'd never fit. She groaned and threw the boot across the room.

"Barefoot it is," she said. "If folks don't like it, that ain't my problem."

Mrs. Pickrin did her hair as best she could, snapped up a black lace bonnet, and dusted off her parasol. She labored down the narrow stairs, stopping along the way.

Lord have mercy.

At the bottom of the stairs, she took a hard look at herself in the mirror.

What happened to you, girl? How could you fall so far?

She could feel her chest and throat tighten. Mrs. Pickrin knew the tears were coming, but she didn't have the time to cry. She had to find her son. It was like a kettle boiling over.

Mrs. Pickrin yarded open the door. She popped her parasol to shield her eyes from the light of day. She shook her head in disgust, unable to remember the last time she had felt the sun on her skin.

Down South Broad she walked, parasol in hand. She could feel the stares from Union troops as they passed, but paid them no never mind. At the Gordon home, she settled onto their front steps to catch her breath. She tried to remember exactly where Johnny's pub was.

Drayton Street? Yes, Drayton Street.

She pulled herself up, popped her parasol, and trudged up Bull Street toward Wright Square. She could hardly recognize it. There, surrounding the monument, was a Union shantytown. Mrs. Pickrin shook her head in disgust — especially when she overheard a Union general flatter a private for his ingenuity for using a gilded mirror for the door of his lean-to.

Disgraceful!

Mrs. Pickrin fought the urge to spit. She turned down President Street (to avoid walking under a Union flag) and then shuffled up Drayton, almost all the way to Bay Street.

The sign on the door read: CLOSED.

Oh, hell no!

Mrs. Pickrin gathered her sleeve in her hand and dusted off the small window to the corner door. She peered in. The bar was trashed. In the reflection of the shattered mirror, she saw the fractured image of a man sweeping broken glass.

Johnny Ray couldn't remember much about how that night ended. After he threatened to report the soldiers, they took it upon themselves to dispense a little Yankee justice. After their lawless disorder, Johnny didn't have much left to his name. When he woke, the liquor was looted, the furniture demolished; it was a wonder they didn't just burn the place down. If it weren't for the fact that Johnny was smart enough to hire a runner to stash the cash, he would've lost the earnings from the prizefight. Not that it mattered. He was going to have it delivered to Mrs. Pickrin to pay for his bothersome conscience.

Blood money, he thought.

Worst of all, he had no idea where the Yanks hid Red's body, and nobody was talking.

BANG-BANG-BANG

Johnny Ray squinted through his one good eye. Silhouetted in the tiny window was the face of a large woman wearing a bonnet. He leaned the broom up against the wall, and then did his best to straighten his disheveled hair. Johnny Ray shuffled over to the door.

"Are you Johnny Ray?" Mrs. Pickrin shouted through the window.

"Who wants to know?"

"Did my boy come to see you?" she said, on tiptoe. "Did Red come to see you?"

Johnny unlatched the door and bowed his head. Without a word, he motioned for Mrs. Pickrin to come in.

"Watch your feet, ma'am," he said. "I ain't quite done sweepin' up. Them bluecoats left quite a mess."

Johnny Ray reached in a satchel and pulled out a thick, brown paper envelope. He set it on the bar.

"I'd offer you a seat, Mrs. Pickrin, but the Yanks did a good job of making my bar standing room only."

"It's okay," she replied. "I don't feel much like sitting," With a quick tug, she yarded off her bonnet. Then, she set her parasol on the bar.

Johnny Ray walked down the bar, sliding the envelope along with him. He couldn't bear to tell her that these were earnings from the fight that killed her son.

"Red wanted me to give you this," said Johnny. "He had been saving up for some time, doing odd jobs for me now and then."

Mrs. Pickrin looked up in wonder.

"There's more'n fifteen hundred greenbacks in there."

"But why did he ask you to hold it."

"You know Red," said Johnny, forcing a smile. "He told me that if I didn't hold on to it, he was gonna spend it all on his mama."

Mrs. Pickrin's lip quivered.

Don't cry in front of strangers, she told herself. *It's not ladylike.*

Johnny Ray looked at his splintered reflection in the shattered mirror, and then looked at his hands.

"Mrs. Pickrin," said Johnny. "I'm awful sorry about Red. I don't know what happened to him, or where he is, but you should know that he got into it with some bluecoats — got into it real bad."

Mrs. Pickrin turned stark white. A shiver ran through Johnny like the cold wind of a Nor'easter. He moved closer to Mrs. Pickrin.

"Oh, no," said Johnny Ray, taking her hand. "He wasn't doing anything that would ruin your good name. Not Red. In fact, I hear tell that he was defending your honor."

Mrs. Pickrin looked up at Johnny Ray. She noticed Red's name scribbled on the elimination chart tacked to the post, just over Johnny's shoulder.

"So he was fighting for the cause?"

Johnny nodded.

Mrs. Pickrin gathered her belongings. She tucked the brown paper envelope under her arm and padded toward the door. Then, she placed a hand on the doorknob. She lowered her eyes. She sighed.

"I wouldn't have it any other way."

According to local legend, the broken body of a brawler was unearthed during renovations at 9 Drayton Street (the former site of Churchill's Pub, now located on Bay Street next to Moon River Brewery) in the 1920s. Rumor has it the coroner had indicated the man died when his neck was broken. (Other versions of this story tell of a mob lynching that took place in the pub, but this is apocryphal, at best. Stringing a man up without benefit of a pre-determined drop won't break his neck, but will result in a slow and agonizing strangulation. The scenario depicted in this story is far more plausible.)

This story originally appeared in Savannah Ghosts: Haunts of the Hostess City – Tales that Still Spook Savannah.

Sweet Tea

3 large Tea Bags
2 cups Cold Water
1 cup Sugar

Ah, sweet tea. You'll never find a more refreshing respite from the dog days of summer.

Pour the two cups water into a pot. Add the tea bags. Bring water to a boil, and then remove from heat. Do not continue boiling. Let steep for 10 minutes. Pour warm tea into an empty pitcher. Add the sugar and stir until it is dissolved. Fill the pitcher with cold water. Hint: for a stronger tea, use less water. Add plenty of ice to the tea instead.

Horse-powered

Dow Harris

November 1910

Rhythmic thunder pounded the earth as Cotton Bob rode high and fast in the late afternoon. His hair blew back from his forehead. He loved the speed of a horse moving at full gallop across an open pasture. Breakneck speed. He spurred Fox, his big red Tennessee Walker, as soon as he saw the cotton field unroll. Cotton. Everywhere the eye could see. An endless sea of cotton. As Fox busted through, bolls flew up into the air, enveloping man and horse in one tumbling white whirlwind.

He was on his way back home to his family's farm near the Tallapoosa. Considering the blistering heat, a swim was in order. He thought about how cool the water would feel. Bob whistled a careless tune through his teeth as Fox accelerated. Usually he walked the distance, in order to better observe the forest and to stretch his legs, but this morning he had gotten up a little late and had had to make double time. It was a fun ride anyhow. It always intrigued him, though, how different his thoughts were when moving at a higher velocity. He thought of principles and airy concepts and bits of poems and dreams rather than the woodland critter details that he tended to focus upon when on foot.

The world seemed to part before the coordinated force of a man and his horse. Horsepower. The archetypal abstraction of dynamic propulsion. He could beat Time itself on a horse. Feeling a little arrogant as the wind tried to prevent his thrust, he thought that perhaps there was no such thing as time. There was only the *feeling of time*. It was relative. Time was consciousness driving itself through the universe at a particular rhythm. That was all. Certain adjustments had a way of, well, wrinkling things up a bit. An hour was a moment and a moment was eternal when you raced the wind.

There was a dirt road at the edge of the field. He swung Fox right just before he crashed through the brush on the other side. Again he spurred the horse for the straightaway up ahead on the bridge above the Tallapoosa River. He would have to slow down when he got to the other side because of a steep curve to the left and so now he really made it count.

As he crossed the bridge, he thought he heard something strange. It was perplexing, something he intuitively grasped before he cognitively realized. Danger! The sound of a loud motor or motors. It wasn't a train. It was a...

Two moving metal blocks appeared around the edge of the curve, coming toward him at a very high speed. He noticed blurry numbers painted on the front of each vehicle. It looked like there were men sitting on them or in them somehow, steering against one another. They had masks and goggles on. They must have been going at least three times faster than he was. There was no room to pass. There was no room to turn around.

He could feel Fox tensing up, ready to bolt in the other direction. The horse suddenly reared up on two legs, fighting against the tight rein. The brightly colored tracers left in the wind behind the approaching machines entranced Bob.

It was obvious that one of the contraptions was trying to slow down. There was smoke hissing from the tires and the driver was swerving. The other one kept barreling forward.

Time stopped and his will became a laser thought telepathically communicating with his four-legged companion. *Jump, you son of a bitch!* He turned Fox's head to the left and let him leap off the bridge and into the deep water below. Time began again and as they dropped towards the cool green, he thought he heard a crash on the bridge high above.

He plunged into the baptismal waters whose sounds had nurtured his youthful wonderings on many a July night. He went down touching the bottom and opened his eyes to darkness. It had been too much for the conscious mind to maintain. Blackout.

When he came to, he heard the crackle of a campfire nearby. There was a dreamlike quality in the air. He picked up the familiar sounds of the crickets and the frogs. And underneath it all was the sound he had forgotten to notice, the rushing waters. He could see nothing.

He sat up and felt a wrenching pain in his lower back, which sent a stinger down his right leg.

"Fox!"

There was a snort and a whinny nearby. Thank goodness.

"Lie still, bud." The voice was grating, nasally – a sure sign of a damned Yankee.

"Horse is fine. Automobile's not. Crashed it into the bridge support tryin' to drive around ya." The stranger crouched next to Bob, cracked open a Thermos, and poured some coffee. He handed the cup to Bob.

"Coffee?"

Bob blindly swatted at the man's greasy hand. Hot coffee erupted from the tin cup.

"Bastards! Flyin' 'round curves like that! 'Bout killed me and my horse!" Bob pressed his palms into his eyes and suddenly realized he was blindfolded. He tugged at the ragged cloth. The stranger placed a firm hand on Bob's wrist.

"Better leave that on. You blew out some blood vessels when you hit the water. It'll go away, but right now, with those red eyes, you look like a freak."

Bob settled onto his elbows. "Who the hell are you?"

"Name's Hughes. Hughie Hughes." He ran a greasy hand over his mustachioed face. "And I was about to blow by that friggin' guinea Pizarro when you came trottin' over the bridge."

"Who?"

"Pizarro. Felice Pizarro. The guy drivin' the Fiat. Blew right by you. Barely batted an eye."

"Is he still around here?" Bob craned his head, unconscious that he was wearing a blindfold.

"No, No. He didn't miss a lick. He's well on his way back to Savannah by now."

"Well, hell, let's go to Savannah then and have ourselves a time!" Bob stood up and yelled in excruciating pain as he put weight on his right ankle. He fell back down.

Hughes laughed at the teenager's temerity.

"You're stuck here, kid. You got a bum ankle. And besides, that speghetti eater will be off to another race in another land before you know it. You'll never get a swipe at him."

Bob didn't say anything. His mind turned to the dinner he was supposed to help his mother prepare for the family.

"Well, kid, since you're stuck around the campfire, maybe you'd like some of this. It'll put hair on your chest." Hughes pulled a silver flask out of his chest pocket and carefully handed it over to Bob.

"What is it?" Bob asked.

"Moonshine. Picked up from an old coot just outside Tallassee at a trade post called *Rance's Shot House* during a pit stop."

"That's my grandiddy's place."

"No shit?"

"Yeah, he made rifles for the Army of Tennessee. They said he was the best *shot* in the county."

"I don't see the connection to moon..."

"Idiot. Gimme that..." Bob grabbed the flask.

He took a deep swig. It sent shivers throughout his body. He still didn't understand what was going on. What kind of business was this feller involved with? He was using some weird words.

The alcohol unleashed his blood instantaneously. He ripped the blindfold off and with the vapors still flowing through his nasal passage; he tried not to miss a beat. His eyes were blazing.

"Hughes, what the hell is an *AUTO-mo-bile*?

Hughes smiled.

"Where've you been for the last ten years, man?"

Cotton Bob didn't say anything. He just took another swig and looked up dreamily.

"We've got a long night ahead of us. Here, give it back!" Hughes sat down on a log next to the curious young man and took his turn.

He gave Bob the brief history of the automobile as best he could between sips of Rance's moonshine. He hadn't realized that there were many parts of the rural South that had never even heard of the motorcar. That would explain all those strange looks he kept getting from farmers and folk he had flown by in the past couple of weeks.

It was an interesting time. Most people across the country still traveled by means of horse and carriage. All of the roads connecting the cities were dirt and most of them were only wide enough for *one* vehicle at a time.

In 1895, the Duryea brothers received a patent for the first gasoline-powered automobile in the United States. P.T. Barnum featured their vehicle in his traveling circus. The motorized freak commanded more attention than all the other exhibits combined. Yet Charles and his brother Frank were constantly fighting over credit for the patent and their models failed to evolve with the competition.

Soon others began achieving renown. The first race in the United States took place on April 14, 1900. Top speed: twenty-five miles per hour. In 1901, the Italian Henry Fournier had been the first to drive a mile in under a minute. A couple of years later, a doctor from Vermont and his chauffeur took the first transcontinental endurance ride. They reached the Pacific in sixty-four days.

Originally seen as a rich man's toy, the recreational potential of the motorcar was exploited through intensive male competitions the world over. This was an exciting, experimental period full of gambling, which inadvertently facilitated the evolution of the industry. A thousand variations of the "horseless carriage" had been racing around for almost ten years. The engines were getting bigger, the bodies more aerodynamic, the speeds higher, and the character of the racecar drivers more reckless and cavalier.

Starting in 1904, W.K. Vanderbilt sponsored a race known as *The Vanderbilt Cup*. This had become the most famous race in the United States. First prize was a $5,000 silver cup made by Tiffany, along with a $2,000 purse.

Hughes was from Trenton, New Jersey, in Mercer County. He had gotten in with the Roebling family there, who had built the Brooklyn Bridge and the Golden Gate Bridge. Just about every major bridge built since carried their patented support cable. On the side, the family began investing in the burgeoning motorcar industry.

Washington Roebling, Jr. was at the helm of the racing side of things. He was a well-to-do intelligent aristocrat with a vision. He had decided to name the company after the county. And it just so happened that Mercer County was named after a Revolutionary War hero who was a direct ancestor of the famous Mercers of Savannah, Georgia. And somehow, Savannah had brought the South into the auto-racing world…

Thick billowy cigar smoke covered the back room of the bar over at the Oglethorpe Club, the preeminent men's leisure organization in Savannah. Nine middle-to-elder-aged Southern gents sat around a long table. This was the Savannah Automobile Club and Frank Battey, the president, had called an emergency meeting. Governor Hoke Smith was also in attendance.

"Who do you think you are, Barney Oldfield?" George Tiedeman, mayor of Savannah, spoke sarcastically to Battey, who now sat back with a smug grin. He lit a fat Havana and proceeded to blow rings. The other men laughed. The piano player in the background began rolling out the Maple Leaf Rag.

"Yeah, he thinks he's Barney Oldfield, all right. Look at that see-gar in his mouth." Major Stephens seconded the motion. Barney Oldfield, the famous circus master race driver, was already a household name in many U.S. cities.

Battey had recently been in touch with key officials of the AAA (Automobile Association of America). Apparently, there had been a bit of a dispute with the ACA (American Car Association) regarding standardization procedures involving European cars. There had also been arguments over holding races in New York. The people there did not like having the roads shut down for the races. And there had also been a number of accidents already involving spectators. This was attributed to the crowded circumstances, but it also may have had something to do with vendors who had gotten away with selling ticklers, bamboo sticks with feathers attached to the end meant to "tickle" the drivers as they zoomed by. But down in sunny Savannah there was plenty of room and no such nonsense. And Battey was 'bout near crazy to get the Vanderbilt Cup to come down.

"Are you trying to tell me, Frank, that you have convinced the bigwig race sponsors in New York City to bring an international racing event to li'l ol' Savannah?" Governor Smith was still incredulous.

"Yes, guv'nah. That is what I am a tellin' ya. Imagine all of the European countries and our Northern brethren convergin' on our enchanted little city to participate in the most extraordinary automobile race ever held in the entire world: *The Southern Vanderbilt Cup*. Ha. Ha. Ha. Ha. Yes. Indeed. The rise of the horseless carriage! The South ain't never seen anything like it!" Battey looked up at the ceiling. The other men laughed again at his boyish demeanor.

T.A. Bryson, first automobile dealer in the South, interjected.

"You always were a dreamer, Frank. This might be just what we need down here to get the industry goin'. I'm in. I'll cover the advertising expenses."

Battey jumped up and raised his glass. His right hand moved back and forth with his voice as he tried to present a mental picture for the others while he made his toast. He took a big puff off of his cigar and blew a cloud above them all.

"The chain gangs will clear the track! The state militia, armed with the ancient bayonet, will guard the way against the intruder! The local farmers will sell fresh produce to visitors from Wall Street as they get off the trains! The live oaks and Spanish moss will offer ample shade and a romantic glade for all the young lovers as they picnic. When the drivers fly around La Roche, they'll see a gorgeous marshscape and maybe a glimpse of Bonaventure cemetery. A hundred thousand from all over the South will flock to Savannah to have a look-see and to cheer them on as they careen down Victory Drive. *Vrooom! Vroom! Vroom!* We'll sell whiskey if it's cold and lemonade if it's hot! And cotton will be floating in the air! We 'gon git that trophy, boys! Vanderbilt won't be able to resist! To the Great Savannah Races!"

Everyone cheered.

Governor Hoke Smith now stood.

"All right, Frank. You've sold me. Let's make it a citywide holiday. Wouldn't want the little boys and girls to miss out on the fun, now would we?"

The campfire seemed to undulate to the beat of the tale. Cotton Bob was fascinated.

"Did they get the Vanderbilt Cup to come to Savannah?"

"Well, no, they didn't. At least not in 1908." Hughes replied. "But they held a number of smaller races and one big one called *The American Grand Prize*. The ACA offered a $4,000 purse and a gold trophy worth more than the coveted Vanderbilt Cup.

"After the races in November of 1908, the sponsors decided to go back to New York. The ACA and the AAA had resolved their differences and thought Long Island might be better after all because of the higher concentration of capital and the greater advertising network. This upset the Savannah car clubs because their races had gotten such a good reception in 1908. It also upset the drivers because the track in Savannah was so smooth and the hospitality of the people so magnanimous.

"So, in lieu of having the event inside of Savannah this year, Frank Battey, decided to sponsor a series of endurance races across the South, beginning and ending in Savannah. He himself had drawn out a rough map of all the known roads through Georgia. It's supposedly the first automobile road map of the state. I've actually got a copy in my pack. Beyond Georgia, it was anybody's guess. Navigation alone is the primary obstacle in finishing the race, much less competing. Cars are supposed to race down dirt roads only fit for horse and carriage. And that's how me and you came head to head on that bridge over yonder."

"Wow, that's one helluva story." Bob was still trying to take it all in. "Do you think the races are going to go back to Savannah?"

"I know for a fact that they are. You oughta come. I'll be there." Hughes rubbed his hands together. "For sure."

"We'll see." Bob leaned back and gazed into the fire...

Bob thought of those cars and how powerful they were and what sort of future might be in store for a fellow who could bring them to a small town like Tallassee. Every time his dad went down to Montgomery, he asked to go so that he could pick up newspapers to see the automobile advertisements and reports of the wild races going on in various parts of the country. The Grand Prize Race in Savannah that year was a humdinger that came down to the last second. But the Vanderbilt Cup had still eluded the Savannah auto enthusiasts.

Bob had saved enough to make the trip and word was that Battey had finally convinced "Willie K." Vanderbilt to let Savannah host the Vanderbilt Cup that year. All of their dreams were finally realized. Bob's dad agreed to let him use the one-horse carriage, so that he could pack enough supplies to make the journey. It took him a week and a half to get to Savannah. He had some close calls with roadsters driving by but nothing like his experience on the Tallapoosa Bridge. Fox had begun to get used to new sounds. Each night, he would find a cool place to camp in the ample forest and fields of central Georgia.

One night he stayed in a peach orchard. The peaches hung heavy and he took it upon himself to pick a few, and then a few more to share with Fox. After drinking some of Rance's moonshine, he leaned back and gazed into the open sky. The stars jumped around twinkling. There were a couple of shooting stars. He dreamed of the Georgia Peach, princess of the South, wandering through the orchards, singing like a nightingale.

"Oh, where have you been, Billy-boy, Billy-boy,

"Oh, where have you been, charmin' Billy...."

He arrived at dusk in the forest city on November 26, a couple of days later, the day before the races were supposed to begin.

He came in on Oglethorpe Avenue and was staring up at an owl perched in the moss-covered tree tunnel when a lady yelled at him to stop. He looked down and realized that she wanted him to yield so that she could cross the street. She was dressed in a flowery pink dress. He tipped his straw hat and brought Fox to a halt.

"My apologies, ma'am. I hope you'll excuse me."

"You boys are always lookin' off in the distance. I do hope you'll be more careful next time."

"Yes ma'am, you're right. It's hard for me sometimes just to keep my feet on the ground."

He jumped out of the seat and stepped directly in front of the lady.

"What's a beautiful woman like you walkin' round without an escort for?"

"Well, I'll be. You are a rude one. Indeed. Escort? What's that supposed to mean?" She brushed him aside.

"Ma'am, I don't mean it that way." Bob tried to catch up and she hustled off.

"Could you at least tell me of a good place to stay for a couple of days? I'm here for the big races."

After a few moments, she looked back and smiled.

"Everybody who's anybody is staying over at the DeSoto."

"Where is it?" He asked politely.

"At the corner of Harris and Bull St. You can't miss it." She turned around and continued walking away.

Bob looked up in the air again.

"Savannah. Thank God, I finally found Savannah."

The DeSoto, jewel of Savannah, was a grandiose red brick Romanesque building that had been unveiled on New Year's Day in 1890. It was by far the most extraordinary hotel in Savannah. Electricity had arrived just a few years before and the DeSoto was decked out with multiple chandeliers and sconces in every room.

On the southwestern portion of the extensive complex, the architect, William Gibbons Preston, designed a wide rotunda. This was the main lobby and public area. In the middle of the circular room was an enormous fireplace, approximately six feet tall. There was a chill in the air and many people gathered here for warmth. The chatter of excited anticipation filled the room. Bob could see the orange flames flickering on their faces as he walked up to the front desk. A Dixieland ragtime band offered a rowdy tune in the background. The pop of the tenor banjo really stood out.

"Yes, ah, I am here for the big races. How much are the rooms?"

The lady in front of him smiled at his naiveté.

"There are no rooms left, sir. Apparently, there are 100,000 people in the city. All the high falutin' folk booked up way in advance. But you are in luck. The DeSoto is opening its doors wide to the visiting public. The city has even opened the jail to guests. They've got the president of Michelin Tire Company in solitary confinement! And he likes it."

Bob was still a bit confused with all of the commotion.

She pulled a small fold-up cot and a pillow from behind the desk.

"If you can find a spot in the back of the rotunda amongst all the others, you're welcome to stay."

"How much for the cot?"

"A dollah."

He grinned, took the cot, gave the woman two dollars, and headed over to one of the sparser corners of the room to set up camp. He found a spot near a window where he could see Fox outside, tethered to a tree. Madison Square. It looked like he was eating some grass near the Sergeant Jasper monument. Night was beginning to come on. He looked out and saw the beginning of a full moon glow.

After getting situated, he wandered into the hotel's tavern. There was a lot of commotion going on in that direction and he was hoping to find out where the Mercer camp was located so that he could catch up with Hughie Hughes, his ol' buddy.

A large group of men were huddling around a tall figure. They were laughing and had been drinking for some time. From the sound of it, they were from different countries. France, Italy, maybe Germany. Bob wasn't too sure. The guy in the center was American. His voice boomed out.

"Yeah, and if you can believe it, the mayor of Thunderbolt, made a public apology."

"Wutta fa?"

"For having the audacity to buy an automobile. The people here thought it was an unforgivable extravagance! Ha Ha Ha!

"Na, ya donna say. Wy eeza dat ta?"

"Why? Damn. You Euro boys sho' do have a different sense of humor." The young American in the center shook his head, blowing him off.

Bob leaned over to the bartender.

"Who are those guys?"

The bartender stopped cleaning out a glass and tried to explain.

"Those are some of the race car drivers. Most of them are staying at individual camps situated out around the track but they know that the press is here and if there's one thing about race car drivers, it's that they all want to put on a good show. That's David Bruce-Brown in the center. He might be the best that ever lived. Comes from a filthy rich family in New York. Dropped out of Yale so he could race cars. Definitely got an attitude."

"Who's that Frenchie next to him?"

"That's Victor Hemery. He won the big Moscow to St. Petersburg race a couple of years back. He also won the first Vanderbilt Cup. Last year, Bruce-Brown beat him by a second and a half, winning the Grand Prize. It was a helluva race. I just heard him say that he was going to do it again. Right before you came in.

"Next to Hemery is Ralph Depalma. Then there's Joe Dawson, Fred Wagner, Louis Chevrolet, Henry Fournier, Felice Pizarro, and Barney Old..."

"Wait, which one is Pizarro?" Bob interrupted the bartender.

"The one talking, tryin' to seduce the young lady over at the table under the sconce. Why, you got a beef?"

"Yessiree, bobtail. I do."

Bob couldn't wait another moment. He stormed over to Pizarro, got his attention, and when the Italian turned, Bob punched him so hard in the face that the man flew back out of his chair.

"You like that, boy?" Bob stood flexing over the Italian as he cringed in pain. Then he kicked him in the stomach.

"That's fer my horse!"

Pizarro crooned an expletive that Bob couldn't understand.

Just then the French man poured an entire bottle of champagne over Bruce-Brown's head.

"Behold, the young master! Defies his mama's express orders to stop racing and go back to school. What an insolent little brat!"

Bruce-Brown pushed Hemery back. Hemery tripped over Pizarro and crashed into the table. A German Benz driver, who was resentful of Bruce-Brown for changing over to the Italian Fiat team, took a swing while Bruce-Brown was trying to get the champagne out of his eyes.

And then it was on. Germans, Americans, French, and Italians, all brawling in the barroom of the DeSoto. And Cotton Bob had set the ball rolling.

He tried to make his way out, dodging chairs and flying bottles. He had settled his score with Pizarro. On the other side of the tavern was a tall lanky man dressed in a plaid coat with a golf cap on. He had a bemused look on his composed face as he watched all of the mayhem run its course.

"Excuse me, sir, but do you know where the Mercer Camp is located?" said Bob.

The calm man smiled.

"I should say that I do. I own all of the Mercer cars."

"You must be Roebling." Bob couldn't believe his good fortune.

"Washington Roebling, Jr. to be precise, my good fellow. Now perhaps you'll tell me why you laid into that Italian."

"He tried to run me off a bridge a couple of years ago. I was just making things right with him." Bob grinned, putting his thumbs under his suspenders. He popped them against his chest.

"So, you're the one. Yes, well, I was aiming to do the same thing. He destroyed one of my cars. Hughes told me all about you."

Bob tucked in his shirt and extended his hand.

"Speaking of bridges, I hear that you had something to do with the Golden Gate Bridge out in San Fran."

"Actually, it was my father. I have to say that I am more interested in facilitating passage across the bridge rather than the bridge itself." There was an existential quality to the man's rhetoric.

"Is Hughes here in Savannah?" Bob turned the conversation.

"He is but I've made sure that he'll stay out of trouble. He's at the camp resting up. I just put him to bed. He's racing tomorrow morning at 7:30. I came here to look for the mechanic but I haven't seen him. I'm about to head back out there. Would you like to come? I'll give you a tour of the track in our new six-cylinder roadster, *The Raceabout*."

Bob nodded his head.

"Let's go."

The cool air smelled of sea salt as Roebling drove Bob down the track on the South side of Savannah. The yellow roadster with black stripes hummed along quietly, almost completely drowned out by the crickets, cicadas, and bullfrogs. The mud flaps kept all of the dust from flying up. It was now dark. Roebling flipped on two big brass headlights. Then he began to accelerate. Bob's imagination thrilled with the speed as the scenery faded into a blur.

They zoomed down Waters Avenue and then dove down through a series of dark forests periodically bursting through onto a series of causeways running over tidal creeks and miles of marsh grass. In the distance, boathouse lights shimmered across the water, twinkling a sincere welcome.

The track was about fourteen miles long. Roebling took a couple of laps just to satisfy Bob's curiosity. What an amazing journey into the twentieth century. *Imagine the possibilities that lay before mankind.* Their conversation turned to the sea.

"I'd also like to build boats." Roebling mentioned. "Big boats. Hotel boats.

"Have you heard of the Titanic?"

Bob shook his head.

"Oh, well. It's going to change everything. Talk about a smooooth ride. It's still under construction. I've got some interest in it, though, and I'll be on it next year for its inaugural transatlantic voyage."

Both men remained quiet for a couple of minutes.

Roebling spoke again.

"Yesterday, during the practice laps, two of our cars got in bad accidents right at this bend. Fellow by the name of McNay, recklessly driving a Case car comes up on a horse and carriage, and causes a pileup. McNay's dead. Barney Oldfield said that McNay had it coming, that he was *speed-crazy*. Lord knows, I am sometimes... Fortunately, none of our boys were hurt that badly, though Joe Dawson was thrown clean out of his car."

They sped down Ferguson Avenue, passing Bethesda, the famous orphanage, and took a right onto Skidaway crossing onto the Isle of Hope. Roebling resumed with a query.

"I hear that the Joneses are hosting a big oyster roast at Wormsloe in honor of Henry Fournier tonight. I have a personal invitation. Would you like to go? That's where all the ladies will be. And, I hear, there will be dancing on the beach later on."

"Lead the way." Bob leaned back and looked up as Roebling turned the car down the long avenue of interlocking oaks. He thought to himself about all the different generations that must've looked up at those beautiful oak trees in wonder. He was in a perpetual state of awe. Dreamland. Savannah.

The rest of the night was as blurry as the scenery had been while Roebling accelerated the roadster. Bob ate oysters till his stomach could no longer hold them. When everyone started dancing, he decided to wander along the beach, somehow bumping into the girl in the peach blossom dress that he had encountered upon arriving in Savannah hours before. He tried to show her how to skip the empty shells across the water like he was fond of doing back home with stones, but she kept trying to hug him. At a certain point he became dizzy with love or alcohol or oysters and for the most part blacked out. The last thing he could remember was the smell of her hair as he tried to protest. He still hadn't gotten to see his friend, Hughes. Sorry, ol' buddy, he thought, as he sank into the oblivion of the Georgia Peach.

The next morning he awoke on his cot in the DeSoto. Everyone else was still asleep. He looked at the big clock above the fireplace. *6:00 A.M.* Good timing. He stood up, stretched, looked out the window. Fox was still there, still munching on grass. He walked out and jumped on the horse bareback. Leaving the carriage behind he kicked Fox into a quick canter and headed south on Bull Street towards the main grandstand.

It was a cold morning and there was a fog settling heavy over the fields surrounding the bleachers. A few people had begun to show up already. The vendors were selling whiskey out of a bottle to help keep people warm, at fifty cents a shot. Bob bought a dollar's worth just for hair of the dog's sake. He gargled it down and shook his head a little bit. His eyes shone bright. Then he took Fox for a run along the track. He passed a couple of boys on horses up in front of him. He dared them to race and they all tore off together. Bob won. Nobody had ever beaten Fox.

He reached the Mercer camp just as Hughes was rolling the car out of the makeshift garage, situated on the marsh just off of La Roche Avenue.

"Howdy, Hughes."

"Bob. Damn glad to see you. Say, you wouldn't happen to know an available mechanic, would you? It seems my boy got into a little altercation over at the DeSoto last night. He still hasn't showed up."

Bob looked a little sheepish, considering his responsibility for all the fighting.

"No, Hughes. I wouldn't happen to know one at all."

"Seems like you did a mighty fine job helping me repair that car a couple years back."

Bob shook his head.

"Get over here and help me paint the number twenty-five on the front of the car."

Thus Cotton Bob got a first hand glimpse of the racecars in action from the mechanic's seat. In those days the steering wheel was on the right side of the vehicle and the mechanic rode along in the passenger's seat on the left. He was there to change tires and to assist the driver should problems arise at any point along the track. The biggest danger, though, was in effectively applying the primitive hand brakes, which directly leveraged the tires. After about thirty miles an hour or so, it was nigh impossible to slow down abruptly.

The Savannah Challenge was a light car race. The cars were smaller then the average stock that would be competing in the Vanderbilt and Grand Prize races. Hughes was pretty confident. There were only seven entries and he seemed sure that, barring the Marmons, the others wouldn't even be able to finish.

He was right. After the first lap he was in fourth place. He struggled a bit with a fellow by the name of Disbrow, driving a Case car, who whipped him for four laps straight. But by the fifth lap he zoomed into first and at the end of that lap Disbrow broke a camshaft. Hughes never looked back. The other Mercer failed to finish. They beat the Marmons by six minutes.

Hughes mechanic had finally showed up and was angry and ashamed that he had missed the race. He was eager to fill his responsibility, however, for the upcoming Vanderbilt Cup and looked askance at Bob.

Bob was thrilled with all the attention after the race was over but he could barely hold himself together. He was still caught between two worlds. He had never gone that fast in his life, even on Fox, and it was a bit unnerving. He gladly yielded to Hughes' mechanic.

There was barely an hour before the Vanderbilt Cup was slated to begin. Hughes didn't get to enjoy his victory very long because the drivers he was competing against next were much more intense. His mechanic had already begun to paint the number six over the twenty-five. Bob slipped away.

His mind was still reeling from the intensity of the experience. Man can overcome gravity, he thought to himself. It is possible to transcend both space and time. The vendor passed with the bottle of whiskey. Bob grabbed him and paid for two more. He slammed them down without a moment's hesitation.

He turned in a complete circle and marched over to the bets counter, which was a modest little table with a checkered cloth. Things were supposed to be subtle regarding this part of the race. Bob was having a hard time with that.

"I'm a layin' a hundred down on Hughie Hughes in the number six Mercer. Man, that guy is gonna whup ass! He's a race car driver!"

The old man with a wicker hat looked at him rudely.

"Aw, nobody thanks he's gon' win. He's drivin' a six cylinder. No one's ever heard of a six cylinder win any race anywhere."

Bob reflected his thoughts for a moment, scratched his head a couple of times.

"Oh, well. Hmmm. You might be right. I never thought about it like that. Who do you recommend?" His eyes took on a crafty look.

"They say that the sure bet is Mr. Bruce-Brown. Depalma's s'posed to win. So Bruce-Brown's got the best odds compared with the rest of 'em. He's Two to one. Course he won the Grand Prize last ye..."

"Yeah, I know all 'bout him. Yale dropout. Spoiled Yankee. Silver spooned since day one. Forget it. Besides. You don't win much if you aren't willin' to take a chance...I...uh...I gotta stick with my friend, Hughie. I'm layin' it down. Hundred bucks."

"Suit yourself. 20-to-1."

"20-to-1," Bob mumbled under his breath. He grabbed his voucher stub and rushed over to the grandstand to get a good view. The whiskey was really starting to kick in and he hadn't even stopped reeling from the previous race. He couldn't believe what had happened. He had tasted the infinite. He had transcended...He could do it again. He would do it again.

Standing up tall, he peered down to the track. They were all in their starting blocks. The red Fiats. The gray Mercedes. The yellow Mercers. The white Loziers. Lozier??? Was that an American car? The firing gun boomed and the seventh annual Vanderbilt Cup got underway. And dreams of the silver trophy cup, a strange holy grail of sorts, danced through the minds of 100,000 wild and crazy spectators and fourteen bloodthirsty hound dogs in metal chariots that exploded with the press of a pedal. They were off!

Bob followed the progress of Hughes in number six down Waters Avenue as far as he could see. The car was kicking up dust in its wake. At a certain point the car and driver sublimated into a mirage. Cotton Bob's third eye took control and the mind's camera began constructing future potentials into feasible realities. He looked back for a moment and caught a glimpse of a tall slender man in baggy pants, plaid, and a golf cap flipping a gold pocket watch open to check the time. Roebling. As the lid's hinge sprang, the gold reflected the sunlight — a moment of blinding brilliance — and then over the bridge and far, far away.

Cotton fields melted into a sea of white clouds. The Spanish moss wept in the trees as they raced by. Ralph Depalma in the Gray Ghost, number ten, led after the first lap. Hughes. Where was Hughes? Damn. Must be the mechanic. One. Two. Three. Four. Five cars drove by before he caught the yellow blur that was the Mercer Raceabout. Hughes' full mask was pulled down and his goggles were intent on staring, bearing down on the car in front of him. What a time it was!

Bob grabbed the vendor on the shoulder as he went by. He was an old black man with a deep bass voice, who had been yelling out the following mantra all morning long.

"Somebody up heeeee-ah, neeeeeeeds a little alky-hall! I got jest da tingy-dingy-doo!"

"Yessiree bobtail, I am that man! I'll take two more shots!" Cotton Bob reached into his pocket and pulled out a dollar and stuffed it into the man's apron.

He then looked south just in time to see the cars disappear into the mirage again. His raised both full shot glasses up in his right hand.

"To Space and Time," he yelled throwing the harsh whiskey back down his throat. He was erupting on the spot!

"Get 'em, Hughie!"

A woman laughed above him. It sounded like a familiar voice. He was too ashamed to look back. Was she making fun of him? He suddenly became conscious of all the spectators around him, 100,000 people. He had never been in such a large crowd before. It was a bit disconcerting. So many conversations. So much energy. His ears amplified into the intimacy of discourse. Some gentlemen nearby were talking over the odds. Clearly, New York Yankees. Maybe stock brokers. Bob tried to listen more closely

"Well, Mulford's a damn long shot. 20-to-1."

"I haven't met anyone that laid his odds."

"But he's American. Better yet, his car's American. For honor's sake. Crap. I bet on him. I'm not ashamed to admit."

"Kinda reminiscent of Wall Street, eh? A corporation has no loyalty beyond the sure bet. Bahhhhhhhhh!"

"These Fiat Corsa S74s are just unstoppable. This is the first time they've raced."

"Wait a second. Depalma's leading in the Mercedes. They've never raced either."

"Did you guys see the Italian Camp?"

"We did. Bonabella off La Roche. They had a big spaghetti dinner over there last night. It was a riot. Felt like Italy."

"How 'bout the German camp?"

"Out at Greenwich. Yeah. I drove out there yesterday morning. Those guys are crazy. There's a German rifle club that's been in the old Plantation House for a couple of decades. They had all the drivers shootin' at anything that moved across the marsh and river to get pumped up for the race. Whooo...Mercedes and Benz... What a combination!"

Just then, over the loudspeaker...

"Ladies and Gentlemen, the number six Mercer has busted a water hose and has exited the race just beyond Isle of Hope."

Bob's hopes fell. He leaned back — a momentary dizzy spell. His hair was soaking wet. What? There went a hundred bucks, down the drain of wishful thinking. He pushed his way up to the men's little conference.

"Excuse me, slick fellers from the city. Ya'll recall what the odds were on the number six Mercer?"

"Who's the driver?" A fellow in a big black top hat looked down through his spectacles and long nose.

"Hughes. Hughie Hughes."

The stiff man squinched his face up into an arrogant little smirk.

"12-to-1."

"12-to-1." Bob ruminated. Something didn't sound right. The man at the ticket center had said...what was it? He began to shuffle through his pocket for the voucher stub.

The other men resumed their conversation.

"Well, the Loziers are the only American entries left in the race."

"Hey. If one of them comes through it will be the first American win for the Vanderbilt."

"Yeah, and it would've happened in Savannah. Sweet sunny Savannah."

"No. No. Mulford's 20-to-1. 20-to-1. Not a chance. Depalma. Mercedes. All the way!"

"Unh-unh. Bruce-Brown! Bruce-Brown! Bruce Brown!"

Bob took a step back and zoned out for what seemed like a few moments. He pictured the water running from the engine down to the ground. Hughes. It's over. No. Don't give up. He managed to arouse his attention. He imagined Hughes' mechanic trying to tape up the hose. Not today. One win is enough.

Mulford zoomed by him in the number eight Lozier, passing Depalma in the Mercedes. These two dueled for the rest of the race. Near the end of the thirteenth lap, Mulford had achieved a three-minute-forty-seven second lead...

How many thoughts could occur to one in the space of a second? Five? Ten? Or was there even a limit. Information will flow. It all depended on how fast one was moving. Speed is a relative property but victory is an all-consuming absolute.

Mulford got a tire change on lap fifteen. When he zoomed off from the tire tent out on Whitefield, he forgot to put an extra spare on. So at the next tent over on Shipyard, he had to make another stop. An inexcusable error. Depalma was right behind him, gaining at every second. No time to spare. The Green Flag. One lap to go.

In that crucial moment, Ralph Mulford became a true race car driver.

His determination to beat the Gray Ghost was palpable. People sensed his intensity. On that final lap, he turned it up and went...*over the limit*. Despite the brief shift in momentum with his double stop, Ralph Mulford tore across the finish line, overcoming the unbeatable odds and achieving the first American victory in the Vanderbilt Cup.

The crowd went wild! An upset. A newcomer. A Cinderella. Everyone flooded off the bleachers and down to the Victory Circle. The commotion brought Cotton Bob back to his senses. He looked down at his hand holding the creased voucher marking his wager.

20-to-1. 20-to-1 it said. *Wait! 20-to-1?* Those were Mulford's odds. The clerk had given him the wrong ticket. He had mistaken Mulford for Mercer. Crazy old man. He thought there was something familiar about that 20-to-1. Cotton Bob had just hit the jackpot.

"Whooooooo-hooooo! He jumped up in the air, scarcely believing his good luck

He rushed down towards the white number eight Lozier. Ralph Mulford had already gotten out of the car and with a big goofy grin had accepted the glistening silver trophy. He raised it over his head and began turning in circles. World champion. Bob couldn't believe it.

Then behind him. The familiar voice. Velvet. Peach blossom dress. The laughter of the mysterious young lady he had begun to get to know so well over the past few days. He turned around just in time to see her running towards him. Her arms opened wide. He began to smile. Time shifted gear into the slow motion of romance. He rushed to meet her. As he did, he realized that her eyes were focused a hair to his right. She didn't want him, anymore. She swerved by Cotton Bob and made straight for the goofy looking racecar driver brandishing the big silver trophy high in the air. She was after that trophy.

As Bob watched her pass, he whispered just loud enough for her to hear.

"What is your name? Just tell me your name."

The lady heard him and she briefly turned a mischievous eye towards him and smiled as she rushed by.

"Savannah. My name is Savannah...."

The Tallapoosa River carried man and horse at least two miles downstream, transporting him through the shadowy, tantalizing world of the waking dream." He began to wake up fully as he felt the rocky floor of the riverbed near the shore.

The world certainly operated on a very strange network of cause and effect. It seemed like he had been gone for years. He scratched his head and tried to piece together what had happened on the bridge. He was glad to be alive. Fox was already in the yard of his family's farm, munching on grass. He remembered hearing a crash on the bridge back a ways. He hoped that no one had gotten hurt. He stood up on the other side and walked towards the kitchen. The smell of cornbread and beef tips. Dinnertime.

For some reason, he thought he might ought to quit his job at the mill and see about opening up an automobile dealership, the first one in Tallassee.

He stuck his hand in his pocket. What was that big lump? He pulled out a wet wad of one-hundred-dollar bills. He counted out twenty.

Victory Drive was the home stretch of the Savannah Races, hence its name. Some mistakenly believe the palm-lined boulevard was so named to honor veterans returning home after the "war to end all wars." However, in 1927, the City of Savannah honored the veterans of World War I by planting palm trees along Victory Drive. The confusion is understandable.

Old-Fashioned, Savannah Style

2 oz. Bourbon
2 dashes bitters
1 splash branch water
1 tsp. sugar
1 maraschino cherry
1 orange wedge

In an Old-Fashioned glass, mix sugar, water, and bitters. Drop in a cherry and an orange wedge. Muddle into a paste using a wooden pestle. Fill with ice cubes. Pour in the bourbon. Serve with a swizzle stick.

This drink was invented in the 1890s at the Pendennis Club in Louisville, Kentucky, for Col. James E. Pepper, a member of the club whose grandfather, in 1776, opened the distillery that still bears his name. (The label proclaims that the 100 proof Bourbon was "Born with the Republic.") Legend has it that Col. Pepper requested that the Old-Fashioned be made with branch (or bottled) water instead of tap water.

Bolito

David Harland Rousseau

Summer 1956

Mary fanned herself with the rapid rhythm of a humming bird's wings. Lord, it was hot in that tiny church, with everyone packed in so tight. And it sure didn't help that she was sandwiched between big ol' Aunt Flossie and her even bigger Uncle Early.

Flossie stopped fanning herself just long enough to lean in and ask Mary a question. From behind the crinkled church bulletin, she whispered.

"How old are you?" she asked.

Mary blew a puff of air, trying to shoo the feathers from Flossie's hat away from her face. She squirmed a little.

"Ain't you gonna answer?" said Flossie.

"Can't believe you," said Mary, pursing her lips. "Askin' me a question like that in the middle of the sermon!"

"Had a dream about you, baby," Flossie said. With Flossie, dreams always meant something, even if they meant nothing.

"Hush," said Mary, rolling her eyes. The preacher must've said something great, because Big Early jerked forward and thrust a finger skyward.

"I know that's right!" he said in his raspy voice.

The smooth sounds of the Hammond organ trickled ever so gently into a vibrant version of "We Shall Not Be Moved!" Even Nana Hawkins found herself on her feet and rockin' to the rhythm, her tired hands tapping the pew with a soft syncopation.

Mary was grateful for the hymn, but she couldn't decide if it was because she loved to sing, or if it was because it gave her a reason not to listen to Aunt Flossie. Didn't much matter, anyway. She figured if she had to drown out ol' Flossie, it was best to do it in praise to the Lord.

Church finally let out. Even though it was a July scorcher, everyone was grateful to step outside and breathe air that at least *felt* a little cooler. As folks sought shade under the sprawling live oak, Flossie trudged over to Mary.

"You never answered my question, baby," said Flossie.

"You know good and well how old I am," Mary said. She watched as Flossie leaned on Big Early, using him for support while she pried off her new church shoes.

"If you spent your money on shoes that fit instead of playin' bolito," said Early, struggling under her weight, "you might not have to play 't'all."

Flossie smacked him with a shoe. Grinning, Early put up his arms in self-defense.

"Don't you mock me!" said Flossie, chasing Big Early around the lot. Mary giggled, but tried not to take too much pleasure in the antics of her aunt and uncle. Still, watching

Flossie trying to catch Early while wearing one shoe and wielding the other, well, that was too much to keep inside.

Nana Hawkins sat quietly on a small bench under the oak. When Mary finally looked over, she smiled sweetly at her granddaughter and invited her over by patting a place beside her. Mary smoothed her skirts and sat down beside her nana.

"Chile, don't you pay no mind to Flossie," said Nana, looking into the canopy above. "She always tryin' to find the easy way."

Mary smiled and took her grandmother's hand, cradling it in her own.

"Besides," said Nana, "we all know that her dreams are just excuses to play her some Cuba."

"Mm-hmm," said Mary. "And the worst part about that is if she lose…."

"She try to blame it on you!" they said together.

The two ladies laughed, leaning into each other.

"Murry," said Nana, sighing. "I had a dream about Murkel."

Michael. There wasn't a day since his birth that Mary hadn't thought about her boy. Most days, she just got by. But there were other days when thinking of Michael was too much to bear, and so she spent her days taking care of Nana.

"How long has it been?" Nana asked.

"Too long," said Mary, her gaze turned up to the cross on the church steeple.

And too short a time spent with him, she thought.

Michael was a sharp young man who saw an opportunity to serve his country. More than that, he thought that if he made a career in the Army, he would still be young enough to take care of his mama after he retired from the service. But in

1953, on the day the armistice was signed, Michael stepped on a land mine. The only reminder Mary had of her son was that photograph taken of him right after basic. Oh, he looked sharp in his uniform, sitting in front of the American flag. When Mary asked why he didn't smile, all Michael said was, "I'm a man, now, Mama."

Anybody who played bolito with any regularity saw numbers in everything: in tealeaves, in the clouds, in certain comic strips, but always — and especially — in dreams.

When Flossie asked Mary's age, she was lookin' for a number to play. In Flossie's case, she was asking Mary to play for her. It wouldn't do for Flossie to play Mary's age, since the dream was a sign for Mary and not for Flossie. But now that Nana had the dream of her son, Michael — and on the anniversary of his passing, no less — well now, that meant something.

Nana reached into her white purse and pulled out a weathered five-dollar bill.

"Now I know you ain't one to waste your money," said Nana. She gingerly pressed the money into Mary's hand in such a way as to let her know there was no giving it back. "So I been savin' this here fi'e-dollah, just in case."

Mary bowed her head and nodded ever so slightly.

It wasn't long after church let out that word got around about a fortune-teller who rolled into town over the weekend. Most fortune-tellers would rob you blind and high tail it out of town. But, if you had a soothsayer with any talent at all, you could win big money playing yourself "a piece of Cuba," as the old folks would say. Shoot, if the prize were big enough, you might win more than a week's wages. Needless to say, the gossip at the church dinner that night was centered more on the prospect of winning than on the likelihood of salvation. All the deacon could do was remind everyone that the church would soon be in need of a new roof, and that if anyone were to win, they should be as generous with their winnings as God was in his grace.

Flossie took her husband, Early, to the barbershop on West Broad Street. It wasn't that Early needed the company (she fully intended to leave him there while she looked for new shoes), but she knew that the barbershop was the best place for gossip. If anybody knew where to find this new fortuneteller, it'd be the old men playing checkers inside that barbershop.

"But, baby, I just got my haircut last week," Early protested.

"Then just get a trim," she replied. "Or play checkers, or do whatever it is that you men do. Just get me the name of that fortuneteller!"

"But baby, I — "

Flossie stood with her hands planted on her massive hips. Her head bobbed in such a way as to let Early know that a storm was coming, and there wasn't thing one he could do about it. Without saying another word, Early pulled off his cap and ran a calloused hand over his graying hair. Then, with a sigh, he shuffled across the expanse that was West Broad, jogging a time or two to avoid being hit by the big ol' Buicks motoring up and down the wide street. Flossie patted her straightened hair, shouldered her oversized pocketbook, and plodded on.

Sloppy Joe Bellinger was, by all accounts, a big man. Weighing in at a not-so-healthy 425 pounds, it's safe to say he was a *very* big man. Still, Joe Bellinger had the respect of his community. Sure, people knew that he ran numbers and whiskey, and there were even a few folks who said Joe had his hand in managing the ladies working in the oldest profession, but they also knew that when a church or school needed some financial help, Mr. Bellinger was the first one there to write the check, and there were more than a few families who were touched by his generosity.

The big man mopped his brow. Though he had oscillating fans in just about every corner of the room, he was also busy double-checking the day's receipts and couldn't afford to have them blown all about. He even instructed his bookie to walk slowly by the desk as he updated the numbers on the chalkboard behind him.

"How we doin' today?" Joe asked.

"Same numbers keep comin' up," said the lean man. He stepped back from the board and scratched his head.

"Easy enough, Charlie," said Joe, blotting his brow. "Must be a fortuneteller."

The door burst open, threatening to blow the papers from Sloppy Joe's desk. Joe and Charlie, the lean man, glared at the breathless, skinny kid.

"Boy! You must be out your damn mind!" shouted Charlie.

"It's the police!" said the boy.

Joe calmly moved aside a stack of receipts and looked at his stained desk calendar.

"Right as rain," said Joe.

He carefully returned the stacks back to their places and slowly stood. Without a word, the lean man handed him a cigar box secured with a heavy rubber band. Sloppy Joe straightened his tie as best he could and trudged through the swinging door to the warehouse that was his nightclub. The policeman's knock echoed through the dancehall. Joe slid open the peep hatch to make sure that it was, in fact, the police. Numbers running was a very aggressive business. Some days — most days — it was better to have the police at your door than your competition.

Joe opened the door and stepped out onto the loading dock of the warehouse. The freckle-faced kid in the policeman's uniform tipped his hat to the big man, who smiled warmly in return.

"Mr. Bellinger?" said the young cop.

"You seem a little nervous," said Joe. "Rough day?"

"No, sir," said the officer. "First day flying solo."

"Well," said Joe, handing over the cigar box. "If you need anything, you just let me know."

The young officer tipped his hat again and scurried off to his patrol car. Joe waited until the cop was just about to his cruiser.

"Officer!" bellowed Joe.

The cop wheeled around.

"You're doin' just fine!"

The young cop smiled, climbed into his cruiser, and sped off, completely unaware of the wad of bills stuffed in that little cigar box.

"Mister Bellinger!"

"Yeah, kid?" Joe watched the cruiser pull out of the driveway and turn onto West Gwinnett Street.

"You know Miss Mary?" said the skinny kid.

"I know a lot of Marys," said Joe with a chuckle.

"Miss Hawkins."

"Sweet gal," said Joe. "Never see any business from her, though."

"You did today!"

Sloppy Joe cast a sidelong stare at the skinny kid.

"What number she play?"

"Thirty-fi'e."

"Thirty-five...."

Sloppy Joe cracked the Venetian blinds and smiled. The parking lot outside his nightclub practically overflowed.

"It's gonna be a good night, gentlemen," he pronounced to the small entourage packed in the back office.

Joe looked over to the lean man who was busy stitching a small burlap sack.

"Charlie! Make sure you stitch that ball in there good and tight," said Joe. "Right there in the corner!"

Sloppy Joe looked up at the clock on the wall.

"Let's do this," he said, grabbing a bucket of numbered ping-pong balls.

Flossie shoved her way through the crowd. Something told her that tonight was her night. It better be. She paid that no good fortuneteller ten dollars to give her a winning number. Then, just to double her luck, she played it backwards and forwards. See, that was the crazy thing about numbers. If someone was born in the year 1925, you could play twenty-five or fifty-two. You could even add all those numbers together and get seventeen, or just seven. It all depended on your point of view. In Flossie's case, she was told that forty-three was the winning number, but she also knew that everyone in Carver Village and in Cuyler-Brownsville was playing some variant of forty-three — at least those who listened to the soothsayer. So, in her hand, she clutched not fewer than four receipts, all based on the number forty-three.

The door to the office opened, and Sloppy Joe and his entourage climbed up on the riser. Joe raised his hand and a hush fell over the crowd. The driving sound of four-bar blues, muffled by the walls of the nightclub, filtered into the back room where everyone waited for the game to begin.

Without saying a word, Charlie opened the burlap sack and watched as Sloppy Joe poured the bucket of marked ping-pong balls into the bag. The crowd strained their necks to witness the tying of the bag. The lean man tossed the bag to Joe, who threw it into the crowd. Around the room it went, from person to person, saluted by cheers and the occasional epithet. Eventually, the bag was hurled at Sloppy Joe who clumsily caught it. He then gently tossed it back to Charlie. Charlie caught the bag by the corner and held it up for all to see. Then, in dramatic fashion, the lean man quickly wrapped a bit of twine around the ball he caught. Once he and Joe were satisfied that there was only one ball tied off, and that it was secure, Sloppy Joe pulled out a pocketknife and slit the bag open. A numbered ball fell into his thick hand.

"Thirty-five!" proclaimed Joe, holding the ball aloft.

"Oh, hell no!" said Flossie, tearing her tickets to shreds.

The room emptied about as fast as it had filled up. Shredded tickets littered the floor. It was all Joe and Charlie could do to keep from laughing.

"Guess I'm gonna have to deliver the winnings myself," said Joe.

"I sure do love that new dress, baby," said Nana, taking Mary's arm. "It's such a lovely shade of blue."

"Thank you, Nana," said Mary, beaming broadly. "I sure am proud of it."

The ladies made their way up the steps to the door of the little white church. Another Sunday spent with Nana.

"Wasn't blue Murkel's favorite color?"

"Yes, Nana," Mary said. "In a way, he bought it for me."

The greeters smiled and nodded at the ladies as they passed through the wide doors.

"The dream?"

"Yes, Nana. The dream."

"I thought it was awfully p'culiar, since Murkel died in '53," said Nana. "Did you play fifty-three?"

"No, Nana," said Mary, helping Nana settle onto the cushioned pew. "I played thirty-five — the year my baby was born."

"Sloppy Joe" Bellinger was tried in 1958 for numbers running and other charges. His case made national headlines when Sloppy Joe would fall asleep during the trial. His attorney, Ralph Crawford, contended that it was impossible to properly prepare a defense for his client due to this "Pickwickian Syndrome" and managed to secure his client's freedom.

When Bellinger died, over 2,000 people attended his funeral. Most remembered Mr. Bellinger for his boundless benevolence, since he freely gave to numerous charities, and personally assisted many black families.

Mojito

3 fresh Mint Sprigs
2 tsp. Sugar
3 tbsp. fresh Lemon Juice
Crushed Ice
1-1/2 oz. Light Rum
Club Soda

In a Collins glass, gently muddle the mint with a pestle and coat the inside of the glass. Add the sugar and lemon juice. Stir thoroughly. Pack the glass with crushed ice. Add rum. Top off with chilled club soda. Garnish with a lemon slice and a mint sprig. (Note: don't worry with stirring or mixing. The carbonation of the club soda will do this for you, naturally.)

Since bolito *began in Cuba, we thought it best to complete the circle by offering a drink recipe originating in old Havana:* el mojito.

This sweet, refreshing drink, thought to have originated in the famous La Bodeguita del Medio, *actually dates back to the late 1800s, when Cuban slaves working the sugar cane fields drank sweetened water mixed with unrefined rum. By the turn of the century, the working-class around* Playa de Mariañao *adopted the drink, adding a garnish of lemon and a mint sprig, but that hard-drinking Hemingway would lend notoriety to the drink sometime in the mid-1940s.*

Dry Spell

David Harland Rousseau

Summer 1957

The rain held back again. In fact, it hadn't rained in so long, folks started wondering whether they'd ever see another drop hit the cobblestones. None of that bothered Bobby, though. Those sultry summer nights made it so easy to sleep in the squares.

Bobby's buzz wore off shortly after sunset, so he made his way down Bull Street to Chippewa Square and flopped onto a bench near the walkway across from the Savannah Theatre. Bobby didn't care much for the theatre's relatively new Art Deco style. The stark lines seemed a little sterile to him, and he preferred the traditional brick of the Preston Armory or the DeSoto Hotel just a block or two away. Besides, the buzz and the glow from the neon lights got in the way of his napping.

He looked over his shoulder and glanced at the title on the marquee: *A Hat Full of Rain*. Bobby shrugged. He didn't know much about the movie. He just hoped it would bring 'em in. He pulled off his porkpie hat and set it crown down on the bench. Then, he plucked a harmonica his breast pocket and started to polish it off with a red bandana.

What'll it be tonight, he thought. *A little Dixie, perhaps? Some gospel, maybe? Might could play me some blues....*

It was always a gamble to play the blues, he thought. Savannah blue bloods didn't much care for it — at least not publicly — and that cut into his tip money. As he starting belting out "Blues Before Sunrise," he thought, *at least it ain't none-a-that rock-n-roll.*

Moviegoers trickled through the square on their way to see *A Hat Full of Rain*. Some stopped to marvel at Bobby's harmonica styling and found themselves clapping along with the rhythm. Some tossed a handful of coins into the hat as they sauntered by, while a shamefaced few scurried on by without so much as a passing glance.

"Hey, Bobby."

Bobby looked up from his playing and saw a slender, sharp-dressed man in a fedora and horn-rimmed glasses.

"Hey, Tom! Been meanin' to drop on by," said Bobby. "Got a story for you."

Tom worked for the *Savannah Morning News* and was considered by just about everyone to be a natural born journalist with a real nose for news. Tom liked Bobby, mostly because Bobby told it like it was, and was completely open about everything — especially his love for drink.

A couple of dollars landed in the porkpie hat.

"Thanks, Tom," said Bobby.

"Come on by the office sometime next week," said Tom. "Can't wait to hear the story."

Bobby nodded and got back to playing.

After everyone had settled into the theatre for the movie, Bobby counted his money: four dollars and fifty-seven cents.

"I might even get me a sandwich!" he said, smiling. *Nah*, he thought. *I can get me a sandwich at the soup kitchen.*

Bobby wandered over to the package shop a couple of blocks away. A moment later (and a couple of dollars poorer), he emerged with a bottle of red wine tucked into a brown paper sack. Down to the river he went, quaffing the wine along the way.

The evening passed quietly, and Bobby eventually stumbled back to his favorite bench in Chippewa Square. When the spinning wore off, he took shelter on the white marble bench at the north end of the square. The high-backed stone bench offered a bit more protection than the slatted benches that dotted the square. He curled up, bottle in hand, and drifted off to sleep.

Tap. Tap-tap!

Bobby grunted. He felt the tapping on the sole of his shoe, but wanted to go on dreaming.

Tap. Tap-tap!

He raised his head ever so gently and peered through the crook in his arm. There, haloed by filtered sunlight, stood a young man in a smartly pressed uniform.

"'Bout time y'all got here," said Bobby, easing himself up. "I could use a good cup-a-Joe."

The court proceedings were pretty straightforward. Anybody who was picked up for public drunkenness (or related offenses) found himself in the hoosegow to sleep it off for thirty days. That didn't bother Bobby much, neither, doing time as a Bay Rum Cadet. He knew most of the cops by name, got to dig up the dirt and dish it out to his buddy, Tom (who would then front him a couple of bucks here and there). He didn't even mind having to sit through hours and hours of listening to social workers extol the virtues of moderation and abstinence. In fact, Bobby made a game out of it — a sort of mental drinking game. Every time a well-meaning Social Worker would utter some catch phrase, Bobby would take an imaginary drink. Bobby couldn't decide whether the hardest part of the game was keeping a straight face or not mouthing the mantra along with them. He'd been in and out of the yard so often; he could practically give the lectures himself.

Days passed, and Bobby saw the same familiar faces in and out of the cop shop. Some "winos" answered phones or helped with the filing. Others emptied wastepaper baskets and mopped floors or picked up litter, but all yard birds had to take up some chore to serve out their thirty days. As for Bobby, he liked being outside and preferred washing the patrol cars parked in the lot behind the barracks just up the street from the jail. There, he had time alone to think. Every once in a while, he'd solve the world's problems with an officer waiting to take the cruiser out on patrol.

Bobby squeezed a sponge of soapy water over the windshield and watched the bubbles roll down the glass. He found himself staring at the dark clouds reflected through the hazy foam and wondered whether the coming rain would ruin his hard work. Lost in thought, he barely noticed that Corporal Jones had wandered up.

Over the past month or so, Corporal Jones had taken a liking to Bobby. It seemed that, unlike so many others (including some of his colleagues), Bobby had a real feel for the news of the day and could discuss anything from art to zoology. And,

Bobby never pointed the finger at anyone — including himself — for his "situation."

"Got the stare, Bobby?" he asked. Bobby shook it off, like a hound coming in from the rain.

"Sorry," said Bobby, taking the sponge to the car. "You know how it is."

"I imagine you've got a lot on your mind," said the corporal. "This is your last day, you know."

"Yeah," said Bobby. "But actually, I was thinkin' about that new car Ford's got."

"The Edsel?"

"Yeah."

"Can't say I know much about it. All the ads show is some car wrapped in paper, and about how it's supposed to be the YOU car." Corporal Jones cracked open his Thermos and poured himself a cup of coffee.

"I don't drive, myself, for obvious reasons," said Bobby, scrubbing down the car. "But you watch. That car will be a miserable failure."

"How so?" asked Jones, sipping his coffee.

"First that name. What the hell is an *Edsel* anyway? I mean, sure, it's named for Edsel Ford, but who cares?" Bobby dunked the sponge and wrung it out.

"Then, those crazy ads. Too much glitz." Bobby pulled the chamois cloth from his back pocket and polished the window. "You watch. People will go into the show room, take one look at the sticker, and walk right out."

Corporal Jones shook out the cap of his Thermos and screwed it back on to the bottle.

"Guess they should've talked to you first, Bobby," he said, gazing at the gleaming finish on the car. "Nice work."

"She's all yours," said Bobby.

Corporal Jones reached in his pocket and pulled out a couple of bucks.

"This is for you," he said, handing the money over to Bobby. "Treat yourself to a nice meal."

Bobby nodded and shook Corporal Jones's hand. Then Bobby opened the door to the cruiser for the corporal. Once he was settle in, Bobby shut the door and waited. The Pontiac rumbled to life.

Corporal Jones watched the first few drops of rain explode on the windshield. He rolled down his window and looked up at Bobby.

"Figures, huhn?" said Jones. "Get the car all shiny and new, and now it rains."

"I reckon we need it though," said Bobby. "It's been too dry for too long."

The heavens opened up, and the first soaking rain in years washed over the Hostess City.

"Get yourself out of the rain, now," said Jones. He turned one last time to look at his newfound friend. "And Bobby, I don't want to see you do another thirty."

Bobby nodded and watched the cruiser roll out of the parking lot and onto Habersham Street. Alone in the parking lot and soaked from the curtain of rain, Bobby looked at the money in his hand and thought of all the ways he could spend it. All he could think about was how good that next bottle of wine would taste, and about how good it would be to be washing cars again.

A few years later, the State of Georgia would pass a law effectively eliminating the thirty-day sentencing for drunkenness. Folks like Bobby lost the security blanket of thirty days in the yard and found themselves with nowhere to go. Sadly, this law led to a sharp rise of homelessness in the Hostess City, and throughout Chatham County. As for Bobby, he wandered into the street one day and was hit by an oncoming car. He never recovered.

Shirley Temple

4 oz. lemon-lime soda
2 oz. ginger ale
1 tsp. grenadine
1 maraschino cherry
1 orange slice

Fill a highball glass with ice cubes. Add the grenadine. Pour in the lemon-lime soda and ginger ale. Garnish with the cherry and an orange slice.

This "Kiddy Cocktail" is a good way to let the little ones share in the experience of drinking a cocktail with their elders — without sending the old folks to the hoosegow. It's also a respectable drink for those who don't imbibe, or who drew the short straw to be the designated driver.

Invented at the Royal Hawaiian Hotel in Honolulu, the drink was named for the 1930s child actress, who often stayed at the hotel.

SHIRLEY TEMPLE

Set 'em Up, Joe

David Harland Rousseau

Spring 1988

Sweet Georgia Brown's was buzzing. The Azaleas were in full bloom, and that brought tourists by the bus loads — most of them of the blue-hair-and-foxtrot set. At the request of one of those sweet Midwestern septuagenarians, Joe Odom hustled on over to the grand piano near the bar. With a quick, snappy gesture, he had the regular piano player slide on down. Without missing a key change, Joe eased on in and picked up where the piano man left off. He slowed the tempo down, just a bit, so he could adjust the microphone and still play with one hand.

"Guess I'm just an old music freak," he said, running a finger along his blonde mustache. "So when this little lady — what's your name, darlin'?" Joe craned his neck so he could hear.

"Hanna," came the reply. In her a soft, Minnesotan accent, it came off as sounding like "HAH-nah."

"Oh, darlin'," said Joe with a wink. "I'm afraid I can't quite wrap my southern mouth around that."

He began noodling with the softer, slower version of "Hard Hearted Hannah."

"Mind if I call you Hannah?"

The old lady beamed, and brought her delicate hands to her wizened face.

"Anyone know who wrote it?" said Joe, picking up the tempo a little bit.

The answers came fast and furious.

"Johnny Mercer!"

"Love his songs," said Joe, milking it for all it was worth. "But nope."

"Ray Charles!"

"Nope. But he sure did sing a mean version of it," his patent leather shoe tapped the pedal. "So did Ella."

"Cole Porter!" came a raspy voice from the back.

"You're all good sports!" said Joe, grinning ear to ear. "But the answer I was looking for, for this song, written in 1926, " Joe winked at Hanna. "You're too young to remember, darlin' — is Jack Alger."

A murmur rolled through the crowd as Joe tickled the ivories.

"I remember one time, someone asked me to play 'Rainy Night in Georgia.' I told her I'd do my best to muddle through. It was, after all, *after* my time."

The retiring Minnesotans tittered and giggled as Joe led straight into a very up-tempo chorus with a staccato beat.

"We got a gal here, a pretty, pretty gal here; the meanest gal around!"

The sweet old lady was clapping off tempo with the biggest grin gracing her wrinkled face. Joe flirted with her like there was no tomorrow.

About half way through the song, a lithe cocktail hostess whispered in Joe's ear. Joe listened and — without ever hitting a wrong note — gave a nod to the bartender, a skinny kid with feathered hair.

CLAN-N-NG

The bartender let go of the chord and shouted, "Last call!"

"Well, folks," said Joe. "I've enjoyed playin' for y'all, but you heard the man. Last call for alcohol. I'm gonna turn it on over to my good buddy, Harold, and let him finish out the set."

A portly-but-dapper black man in a white tux eased himself on to the piano bench and started to play "Pardon My Southern Accent." Joe grabbed the mic off the stand.

"Now remember folks, you don't have to go home," he said, cupping his hand around his left ear, as an invitation to the audience.

"But you can't stay here!" shouted the wait staff, in earnest. The gray-hair-and-foxtrot set gathered their coats and made way for the tour bus idling just outside, on Bryan Street.

It was a good night for Sweet Georgia Brown's.

Joe put his white tuxedo jacket on a hangar and walked it to the break room behind the bar. Without bothering to close the break room door, Joe changed back into his street clothes: a tight pair of chinos and a button-down shirt left open. He eased himself into a folding metal chair, slid his aching feet into a well-worn pair of brown-and-white saddle shoes. As he was standing, a buxom bombshell of a blonde stepped around the corner.

"Where ya headed?" she asked.

"Hey, Nancy."

Just about everyone assumed that Joe and Nancy had something going, but it was always difficult for anyone to say for sure. It certainly didn't help that they were on-again, off-again business partners and roommates.

"That man came by again," she said, leaning against the door.

"I know," said Joe, grinning. "I took care of it."

"How so?"

"He asked for a check for the rent, and I gave it to him." Joe kissed her on the cheek. "Gotta run. Company's coming."

As Joe scooted around the corner of the bar, he heard Nancy say, "Tell me it ain't one of them rubber checks!"

"Not unless your account is overdrawn," he said with a wink and a bow.

By the time Joe hoofed his way back to Lafayette Square, he found a party already waiting for him, just inside the gates of the Hamilton-Turner House. Joe smiled and waved. The motley gathering, comprised mostly of members of the service industry and a handful of daring travelers, waved back enthusiastically.

"My, my," said Joe, easing his way through the growing crowd. "3 A.M., and the party's just starting!" He fumbled for his keys, which was mostly for show, since he never really locked the door. Truth be told, he was squatting — this time, legally.

"Well, folks," he said, swinging the door wide. "Don't let me hold you up! Get on in here!"

Before Joe could pour the first drink or play the first tune on the imposing grand piano, folks were making themselves at home. A young couple, regular partygoers at Joe's, scampered down the hall to Joe's bedroom. Joe peered down the hallway and smiled.

"Guess I've got the couch tonight," he said with a grin. "Won't be the last time, I'm sure."

A knock at the door made Joe cock his head.

"Now who doesn't know *not* to knock?" said Joe, striding over to the door, drink in hand. He cracked the gauzy curtain and peered through. Standing on the portico was a tall, dark haired man.

"Well, I'll be," said Joe. He opened the door wide. "Come on in, man. Thought you'd never make it."

John slipped a thin notebook in his back pocket and firmly shook Joe's hand.

"Wouldn't miss it for the world," said John.

"Help yourself to the bar," said Joe. "Everyone else is."

Joe led John into the parlor, where folks lounged on anything that would even remotely pass for furniture.

"Hey, everybody!" said Joe, his hand on John's shoulder. "I want you to meet Johnny B. He's writing a book on us!" Some nodded politely. Others went back to making out with their dates. Joe left John to mingle and moved on over to the piano. He set his drink on a lace doily and practically shoved a pair of lovebirds off the bench.

"If y'ain't playing the piano make way for folks that do!"

3:30 in the morning, and there was Joe at the piano, master of his universe, king of his — well, his "cousin's" — castle. It was hard for anyone to say when the last time was that this slick-talking lawyer from li'l ol' Claxton, Georgia, actually paid rent anywhere, to include the rent on Sweet Georgia Brown's. He stalled eviction by filing a lawsuit, charging fraud against the owners of City Market. Odom claimed they were responsible for financing the renovations to the building in which Sweet Georgia Brown's stood. Joe didn't care if the suit was thrown out.

Ah, what the hell, thought Joe. *That's what Chapter 11 is for.*

Joe loved his new digs and all of her sobriquets and accolades: *The Charles Addams House*; *The Grand Victorian Lady*; the first house in Savannah to have electricity; the inspiration for *Disney's Haunted Mansion*. Joe used them all when tourists were traipsing through this château gracing Lafayette Square. In reality, the mansion was built in 1873 for Samuel Hamilton, the president of Brush Electric and Power, and was later owned by Dr. Francis Turner, an osteopath best known for tooling around in an electric car long before such a thing was practical or fashionable. Such stories helped fill the tip jar, and it didn't matter to Joe that they were, in fact, true.

This was Joe's fourth residence in as many years. The last place he occupied was just a few blocks away — a row house near Pulaski Square. That place he had to leave under cover of darkness. It seems that the landlord was due back on the following day. Fortunately for Joe, he didn't have to wait long to find a new place. He was put in charge of managing the mansion-turned-boarding-house-turned-tourist trap, and he rewarded that gesture by throwing lavish (if not scandalous) parties at all hours of the evening — and tonight was no exception.

Somewhere around 5 A.M., those who weren't nodding off were trickling out the door. Joe grabbed a throw and threw himself onto the sofa.

All is well at the Hamilton-Turner House.

Later that day, about half past noon, Ilse Etzel put her hand on the gate to the Hamilton-Turner House, just above the sign which read: *Private Residence: Tours 10:00 A.M. to 6:00 P.M.* Most Savannahians couldn't believe Joe's audacity. After all, there just wasn't much to see and, behind the not-so-closed doors of the Metropolitan Planning Commission, the Downtown Neighborhood Association was putting up one hell of a fight to enforce the residential zoning. Still, the tourists knew nothing of this legal wrangling and, after all, who could resist the opportunity to see the inside of a Second Empire château, even if it were largely gutted and subdivided?

"I shall go up to make sure we're invited in," said Ilse in perfect German. Ilse was a long-time Savannah resident who loved sharing Savannah's history — and that love was certainly reflected in the tips she received from grateful travelers. Apart from being something of a local historian, Ilse spoke no fewer than four languages fluently (which didn't count French, a language she thought was "fussy"), making her very popular with European tourists who visited the Hostess City. So, Ilse reassured her German guests (all of whom spoke perfect English, but found it a delightful surprise to hear their native tongue spoken by a Savannahian) and climbed the portico steps.

Inside, Joe could hear Miss Gloria — his housekeeper — greeting Ilse at the door.

"I'm sorry, Miss Ilse," said Gloria, a five-foot-nothin' ball of fire who delighted in wrangling folks in to see the first floor of the house. "Mr. Joe is, shall we say, Indisposed."

Ilse nodded. Whenever Miss Gloria used that particular phrase, Ilse knew that the night before must have been wild.

"Miss Gloria?"

"I'll be right back, baby," said Gloria. "Don't you go nowhere."

Ilse looked at her watch. *Schweinerei*, she thought. She waved and smiled at the Germans, who were also checking their watches. Just then, the door opened. It was Joe. In the time it took for Gloria to answer the door and attempt to turn the group away, Joe had changed out of his street clothes and into silk pajamas and a smoking jacket. In his off hand, he cradled a champagne flute filled with mimosa.

"Now, why don't you folks come on in?" said Joe, beaming. "Join me for a mimosa."

The Germans conversed amongst themselves, then smiled and ambled up the steep steps, where Joe greeted them. He led the group into the main parlor and slid the pocket doors closed.

"I'm afraid I can only show you the main parlor," he said, pouring orange juice into champagne flutes. "We have folks from *Southern Accents* magazine photographing the mansion today, and I'd sure hate to disturb them."

The Germans smiled. Ilse looked around. Miss Gloria was nowhere in sight. In reality, she was busy trying to hustle the late-sleepers out the door, to no avail. The best she could do was to rouse them from their stupors.

It took all of twenty minutes for the cozy group to hear Joe belt out a couple of Johnny Mercer songs and finish their mimosas. Joe stood up and, as a courtesy, offered to refill their glasses.

"Are you sure I can't interest you in another round?" he asked. "You know it's always after the *next* drink when things get interesting!"

Ilse smiled and opened the pocket door, just in time to see a young lady, wrapped in little more than a bed sheet, saunter down the hall way. Quickly, she closed the door. Just as she was about to take Joe up on that offer for another round, the pocket door flew open. A tousle-haired redhead, stilettos in hand, leaned on the door.

"Thanks for a wonderful time, Joe," she purred. The Germans smirked and whispered amongst themselves. It was evident that Miss Gloria's hard work in rousing the quick and the dead was finally paying off, just a little too late. From all corners of the house they came, in various states of dishevelment, all of them thanking Joe for his hospitality. Oddly enough, it wasn't Joe who was embarrassed by all of this, nor was it the Germans; it was Ilse.

"I think I will have that drink," she said, to the delight of all. "But may I get it *to go*?"

Joe opened the door to a small cabinet. He reached under and pulled a short sleeve of red plastic cups.

"Now, I don't want y'all to think less of me just because I'm offering you plastic," said Joe as he filled the *go cups*. "As much as *I'd* love for you to be walking around the Hostess City in style carrying these pretty drinks in that fine crystal, city council just won't allow it."

The bewildered Germans whispered back and forth. After some debate, one stout, gray-haired gentleman asked, "It is legal for us to drink?"

"Oh, sure," said Joe, smiling. He offered the cup to the grinning German. "Just as long as you're using the magic cups, here..."

Joe leaned in and whispered conspiratorially, "...and don't tell anyone where you got it." The German replied with a nod and a wink.

Soon, the grateful guests cradled their bright red plastic cups with such reverence as to make one believe they were embracing the Holy Grail. One by one, the Germans made their way out and waited for Ilse in Lafayette Square.

"Well," said Ilse. "Once again, I thank you for your welcome, which was cordial, and for your cordial, which was welcome."

Especially today, she thought. She took a sip. She smiled.

"Can I steal that?" Joe said, beaming.

"Might as well." Ilse moved down the steps, waving "farewell."

And with that, Joe waved to passersby, and then closed the door.

The Hamilton-Turner House is now a luxurious bed and breakfast, with sumptuous suites and well-appointed rooms.

Sweet Georgia Brown's is little more than a fond memory. It closed on July 23, 1989, for failure to pay rent.

Joe Algerine Odom died in 1991, and is buried in his hometown of Claxton, Georgia.

Grand Mimosa

5 oz. Champagne
1/2 oz. Grand Marnier®
1 oz. Orange juice
An orange slice

This popular cocktail is a sweet remedy for that harsh morning after. Into a champagne flute, pour the orange juice, Grand Marnier®, and, lastly, the Champagne. Garnish with an orange slice.

Prince Philip, Duke of Edinburgh, said of the Mimosa: "The champagne definitely improves the orange."

The Ritz Hotel in Paris gets the credit for this one, serving it somewhere around 1925. Ever since, it has delighted first class air travelers, early wedding guests, and brunch aficionados. Some folks think that Orangina® makes for a better Mimosa, but who can beat the taste of fresh squeezed? Fresh out of Grand Marnier®? Use Triple Sec or Cointreau®, or leave it out all together.

Incidentally, it's only called Champagne if it originates in Champagne, France. Otherwise, it is a sparkling wine. Lest we be so hasty to condemn the French as snobs or regional purists, we do the same thing in this country with whiskey distilled in Bourbon County, Kentucky, and have since 1789.

GRAND MIMOSA

On *Go Cups*

For a city that had spirits listed as one of its first four prohibitions, Savannah is one of two cities in the United States allowing pedestrians to carry *Go Cups*. The other is the *Big Easy*.

Now I admit, strolling along Rousakis Plaza with a bright red plastic cup filled with your favorite adult beverage is something out of the ordinary. Most bars keep their *Go Cups* within easy reach, so you can often help yourself — once you've settled your tab, of course. (Some bars don't even give you a choice. They serve everything in plastic.)

If you are new to the Hostess City and want to experience this for yourself, these are the rules regarding *Go Cups*:

1. All beverages must be in a paper, Styrofoam, or plastic cup.

2. *Go Cups* can hold no more than sixteen ounces.

3. *Go Cups* are only allowed within the Historic District. (River Street to Gaston Street. Martin Luther King, Jr. Boulevard to East Broad Street.)

4. Only pedestrians may use *Go Cups*. (In other words, don't drink and drive.)

5. For heaven's sake, properly dispose of your cup. Plastic and Styrofoam are not landscaping elements meant to adorn the azalea bushes.

Now I will say there is perpetual and perennial debate as to whether to keep the *Go Cup*, but it would be a crying shame to see it go. At the risk of repeating myself, there is something so very satisfying about sipping spirits in the squares beneath a curtain of Spanish moss.

Cheers!
DHR

Pubs Review

"It's more fun to eat in a pub than drink in a restaurant."
Molly MacPherson

When my colleagues and I began the vetting process for this review, we first had to answer the question, "What makes a Pub?" That's a tall order in a sociable city that lays strong claim to English and Irish heritage alike. The short answer found in the dictionary is that a pub is a bar that may also serve food. That old dictionary certainly cleared that up, eh? Still, it does narrow it down considerably from the multitude of restaurants that may also serve liquor, and from the bars that wouldn't dare meddle with their profit margins by serving food. (So what if they can't open on Sundays?) In the end, we all agreed that the first order in any pub (after the half-'n'-half, of course) was that the pub be something of a social hub, a place to shore up friendships, seal deals, or put away the day. Above all, a pub must be welcoming and worry free.

So, with so many fine bars in Savannah, how *does* one choose which get reviews? Our process follows:

1. Pubs must have been in existence for at least three years. (This knocked out a couple of new pubs, which I hope I'll be able to include in future printings. I encourage you discover them on your own.)

2. Pubs must have been owned and operated by the same management for that time. (This knocked out two others that changed ownership or senior management in the months during the review process.)

3. Pubs must show promise of staying open long after the date of publication. (This caused us to completely edit out a review after it was written. Damn shame, too, since that particular hole-in-the-wall had been in operation for over fifty years.)

4. Pubs must be as popular with locals as with tourists. (This knocked out the tourist traps and "locals only" joints.)

5. Pubs must "feel" like pubs. (Highly subjective, yet oddly universal. We know it when we see it.)

6. The building or business itself must have some local, historical significance.

You'll notice illustrated pint and shot glasses at the top of each review, just below the name of the pub. This is the rating for each pub, with one shot being the lowest possible rating, and four pints being the highest. It's encouraging to note that all pubs listed received favorable reviews.

(By the way, the term "pub" comes from the Brits, and is short for "public houses." Raise a glass to the publicans, for without them, we may not have the standardized pint, the half-'n'-half, or a few thousand tawdry toasts. We also wouldn't have the collective memory of every tale told of every fist thrown, every love lost, or every wound healed with a round or two and a slap on the back.)

With that, I present to you this review of Savannah's Pubs and Taverns.

17hundred90

Menu: Full menu. $$$-$$$$
Wine selection: Very Good. $$$
Beer selection: Good. $$$
Liquor selection: Good.
Service: Good.

Funny thing about 17hundred90; it was built in 1820. It's just one of those Savannah curiosities that ranks right up there with Oglethorpe's monument being in Chippewa Square, or the Pulaski Monument standing in Monterey Square, rather than gracing the squares that bear their names.

The inn was, however, originally built as a boarding house and was quite popular with sailors. Still, the inn has had more than its share of tragedy. The man responsible for its construction, Steele White, was killed in a fall from a horse before the building's completion. His once bride-to-be threw herself from the window of what is now room 204, allegedly because of a broken heart — but not for the loss of her fiancé, rather because of her unrequited love for a sailor.

307 East President Street
(912) 236-7122

These stories make 17hundred90 a very popular stop on the walking tour circuit. When I arrived, I found a packed house immersed in the tales told by their guide. Once the crowd cleared, I found myself in a quaint and cozy (if not sleepy) little pub, with all the amenities you'd expect from a nineteenth century abode: exposed brick and wooden beams, fireplaces, wrought iron.

17hundred90 is a chic romantic retreat. It's also a popular place to impress business associates. The rough and rowdy, however, will find it a little too upscale to belly up to the bar.

---

45 Bistro

Menu: Full menu. $$$
Wine selection: Very Good. $$
Beer selection: Good. $$
Liquor selection: Good.
Service: Good.

This hotel has a firm foothold in history. Enterprising entrepreneur, Mary Leaver Marshall, commissioned its construction in 1851. A decade later, hotel manager William Coolidge would be among the first to hoist the colors of the Confederate States of America. Three years after that, General Sherman would toss him out on his ear to make way for his wounded Union troops.

Today, The Marshall House stands as a shining example of Savannah's perpetual preservation and restoration movement. In the late 1990s, a monumental, multi-million dollar renovation was underway — some forty years after the hotel closed its doors. In 2000, the Georgia Trust for Historic Preservation named The Marshall House a National Historic Building.

Today, this, the oldest of Savannah's hotels, is still *the* place to stay when visiting the Hostess City. Hollywood hotshots, business moguls, and political powerhouses, inspired by its grandeur and superb service, all flock to the Marshall House. On any given night, you might just catch a glimpse of the rich and famous enjoying the ambiance of the elegant bar at 45 Bistro.

123 East Broughton Street
(912) 234-3111

Churchill's

Menu: Good variety. Still retains "pub" feel. $$-$$$
Wine selection: Fair. $$
Beer selection: Excellent. $$$
Liquor selection: Excellent.
Service: Good.

While some locals long for the days of the cozy Churchill's that once occupied 9 Drayton Street until its fiery demise in June of 2003, everyone agrees that owner Andy Holmes set the standard for others to follow. The new Churchill's may dwarf its predecessor (it is now nearly 9,000 square feet), but it feels just as intimate. Holmes even imported a thirty-four-foot hand-carved bar from his native England. This handsome work of craftsmanship alone is worth the price of a pint (or two, or three...).

Some pubs might stop there, but not Churchill's. It is easily divided into four different sections: the bar, a dining room (reminiscent of the original), a game room in the basement, and one of Savannah's now not-so-best-kept secrets, the terrace, from which you can see Johnson Square.

13-17 West Bay Street
(912) 232-8501

Another secret: if it's on the lunch menu, you can order it for dinner. This is especially true for that local favorite, The Mad Cow Burger. It may take a little longer, but if you're craving a good burger with a half-and-half, it's worth the wait.

Disclaimer: Some folks reading this book might bring it along and thrust a finger at the above paragraph and demand in an "it says here" tone that they are entitled some thing or another. For heaven's sake, please don't embarrass the server, yourself, your spouse, or most of all me by doing such a thing.

Crystal Beer Parlor

Menu: Great variety. American pub faire. $$-$$$
Wine selection: Good. $$-$$$
Beer selection: Excellent. $$
Liquor selection: Good.
Service: Good.

Local legend Blocko Manning opened the original CBP in 1933 and sold burgers for a dime. Old-timers will tell you that Manning also ran a speakeasy in the basement beneath the restaurant, where beer went for a whopping twelve cents. (The speakeasy has been long since filled in.)

Belly up to the century old Brunswick built bar and marvel at the craftsmanship. Huge, high-backed booths can easily seat a family — or even a baseball team, for that matter — and the walls are graced with photographs and newspaper clippings from the 1930s and '40s.

Friday nights are especially good nights for the CBP, with Buddy and the Beer Parlor Ramblers belting out Dixieland Jazz like it's nobody's business, and there's always a great mix of folks, from wanna-be hepcats and bohemians to workin' class Joes and their families.

The CBP is just a little out of the way, but owners Buddy and Suzanne are committed to preserving the rich heritage of this original American Pub. That plus a thick, juicy burger makes the trip worthwhile.

301 West Jones Street
(912) 443-9200

Kevin Barry's

Menu: Excellent pub faire. Late night. $$-$$$
Wine selection: Fair. $$
Beer selection: Excellent. $$-$$$
Liquor selection: Good.
Service: Very Good.

Any pub that can keep its doors open for a quarter of a century deserves a toast. Any pub that can keep *me* as a customer for a decade deserves another.

Maybe it's the ambiance. Rustic. Homey. Lively. It feels the way a pub should. The building itself, like many in Savannah, has a rich history. Built in 1815 upon a foundation of great cypress trees, the one-time cotton warehouse has survived the Great Fire of 1820, a yellow fever epidemic, and Sherman's occupation. Many of the bluish stones in the structure are actually ballast stones dating back to the very early nineteenth century. Ships would unload these stones and fill their holds with the cotton stored in warehouses along River Street.

Kevin Barry's is also a gathering place, not just for the Irish at heart, but for veterans as well. Tucked away behind the balcony that overlooks the Savannah River sits the Hall of Heroes. Owner Vic Power has made it a point to invite veterans of all ages from all wars to post their "in-country" photos. (Vic is a stand-up guy when it comes to flying the colors.)

Kevin Barry's has also provided live entertainment where, for a long while, there was none. Talented troubadours singing pub standards take the stage seven days a week.

Popular performers like Harry O'Donoghue, Frank Emerson, and Carroll Brown make regular visits, and it's not unheard of for renowned Irish performers to show up and sit in on a set or two.

If that's not enough to pique your interest, their fish and chips are among the finest I've tasted, as is the Irish Potato Soup.

117 West River Street
(912) 233-9626

Moon River Brewery

Menu: Good variety, local favorites. $$-$$$
Wine selection: Fair. $$$
Beer selection: Excellent. Brewed in-house. $$$
Liquor selection: Good.
Service: Good. Nice folks.

The only brewery in Savannah, Moon River occupies what was once the old City Hotel, and is the site of the infamous 1832 duel between Dr. Philip Minis and James Stark.

Seating is comfortable, and patrons can sip on their favorite beer while watching the brewmeister work his magic. And yes, the beer does flow from the tanks to the taps.

There are some popular standards, but the selection that really caught my eye was the Gallery Espresso Stout. Gene and the crew teamed up with the folks from Gallery Espresso (a very popular coffee house located just south of Chippewa Square) to create, as a buddy of mine put it, "two favorite pastimes in one little glass." I'd never thought I'd find myself in a position to recommend a "dessert beer," but the Gallery Espresso Stout is an excellent finish to any meal – provided you like black coffee and dark beer.

21 West Bay Street
(912) 447-0943

Not crazy about dark beer? Can't make up your mind? The friendly folks at Moon River are happy to serve up a sampler of all of their brews for the cost of what some places charge for a pint.

Molly MacPherson's
Scottish Pub & Grill

Menu: Scottish Pub Faire. $$-$$$
Wine selection: Good. $$
Beer selection: Excellent. $$-$$$
Liquor selection: Excellent.
Service: Good.

Sometimes, you just get a good feeling about a place....

Molly MacPherson's opened its doors in July of 2005, and folks have been filing in ever since. It's loyal following grows with every passing week, and travelers from around the globe make a point of marking their hometowns with a pushpin on a map mounted on the wall near the entrance.

311 West Congress Street
(912) 239-9600

Paula Deen fans may remember the days when 311 West Congress Street was the first home of Lady and Sons. Well, the women of the MacPherson Clan and the men who married them have done a fine job of making it all their own. Kilt-clad wait staff serve Scottish favs such as Neeps and Tatties, Cock-a-Leeky Soup, and that perennial pub favorite, Fish and Chips. Nearly three-dozen single malts and about a dozen imports on tap round out the menu, and Molly MacPherson's is the only pub around to offer a midnight happy hour.

AUTHOR'S NOTE: I know. I know. I broke my own rule regarding how long a pub should be in business before getting reviewed, but every now and then, it's a good idea to break the rules — especially if you wrote them.

Pinkie Master's Lounge

Menu: Spicy popcorn.
Wine selection: Poor. $$
Beer selection: Good (especially if you like PBR). $$
Liquor selection: Good.
Service: Good.

Republicans beware: for more than half-a-century, Pinkie Master's has been a democratic — and I'm talkin' yellow dog, Georgia democrat — stronghold. For those of you not in the know, a "yellow dog democrat" is one who'd sooner vote for a yellow dog, than for anyone from any other party — especially republican. Another tidbit: overall, traditionally conservative Georgia democrats bear striking resemblance to moderate republicans (don't tell them that), and might regard democrats from northern climes as "too liberal" (they'll tell you that, unless you're republican).

In his run for office in 1976, former President, then Governor, Jimmy Carter stood on the corner of the bar and declared his candidacy for the Presidency — and on the holiest of high Savannah holidays, St. Patrick's Day. Ever since, a permanently mounted plaque has graced the bar. It reads: "In honor of Jimmy Carter."

Every time I part the saloon style doors, I think back to the days when the men in my family would drag my young, freckled-face self to the VFW. It has that same kind of smell: fifty years of stale cigarettes and spilled beer. You can smell it from the street — or is that nostalgia? Still, you'll find no better place for a cold, cheap beer anywhere in the Hostess City, and you gotta love a bar that takes such pride in its politics.

318 Drayton Street
(912) 238-0447

Planter's Tavern

Menu: Excellent selection. Matches the ambiance. $$$$
Wine selection: Good. $$$
Beer selection: Fair. Bottled beer only. $$
Liquor selection: Good.
Service: Superb. Well-groomed, well trained, yet sociable.

Built in 1771, the Planter's Tavern sits beneath the venerable Olde Pink House Restaurant. In fact, it shares the same menu and the same well trained staff. The tiny room is flanked on both sides by fireplaces lit year-round, even in the doldrums of summer. Don't worry, though. Management keeps the tavern at just the right temperature.

Beer snobs like myself will be disappointed by the limited selection of beer, and might even feel guilty ordering one, but take heart; the bartenders know how to make a mean Manhattan, and there is a respectable wine list to suit the palates of novice and expert alike.

On any given night, Gail Thurmond tickles the ivories, while her sweet, smoky voice fills the room. Couples can curl up on the couch closest to the baby grand and make requests, if they wish.

Most of the crowd was thirty-five and up, with anyone younger than that wearing the familiar glow of the newly wed. It's quite possibly the most romantic tavern in the Hostess City.

1771
PLANTERS
TAVERN

23 Abercorn Street
(912) 232-4286

Six Pence Pub

Menu: Pub faire. $$-$$$
Wine selection: Fair. $$
Beer selection: Excellent. $$-$$$
Liquor selection: Good.
Service: Fair.

A British friend once told me that she liked Six Pence because it reminded her of home: acceptable food and generally adequate service. Ah, you've got to love the self-effacing nature of the Brits.

When I find myself down Bull Street and am thirsting for a Black-and-Tan, I'll pop in to the Six Pence — but only if I have time to wait. That leisurely approach to service has been their M.O. for nearly a decade.

Six Pence is readily identifiable by its wonderfully English exterior, complete with a red phone box (the phone was removed years ago), and the interior takes you back to jolly ol' England. (Be sure to take note of the incredible collection of steins lining the shelves behind the bar.)

The Six Pence packs 'em in. During any late-week happy hour, you'll find 'em stacked, racked, and packed three deep at the bar. Just outside, people-watchers while away the afternoon sipping ale or cider under the shade of patio umbrellas, and who can blame them? Six Pence Pub is a great location for that age-old pastime.

245 Bull Street
(912) 233-3156

The Rail Pub

Menu: Steamed Hot Dogs and Peanuts. $
Wine selection: Poor. $$
Beer selection: Excellent. $$
Liquor selection: Good.
Service: Good.

What do bikers, aging yuppies, and college jocks all have in common? They all hang out at The Rail.

Contrary to popular belief, The Rail doesn't get its name from the steel rail footrest bolted to the bar. The name is a nod to the workers themselves. In the late nineteenth century, day laborers congregated in nearby Franklin Square hoping to "work the rail." Around the same time, a different sort of professional worked the rail: the prostitute. The story goes that 405 West Congress Street was once a popular brothel. In the mid-1990s, owner Melissa Swanson turned this former house of ill repute into a popular pub with a loyal following.

A cozy hole-in-the-wall, complete with no fewer than two fireplaces and a cordoned off darts room, The Rail's no-frills approach is a refreshing change to the hyped up pick-up joints that have over-run City Market – and there's something to be said for a place that has (mounted prominently above the bar) a year-round countdown to St. Patrick's Day.

I'd say that The Rail is a great place to start your evening. As the night wears on, the college crowd packs it in like a frat party in a phone booth.

405 West Congress Street
(912) 238-1311

Venus de Milo

Wine selection: Superb (More than 150 wines). $$-$$$
Beer selection: Good. $$
Liquor selection: Very Good.
Service: Very Good.

Long before wine bars became trendy in Savannah, Shelley rolled the dice and opened Venus de Milo on New Year's Day, 1999 — but not without a whole lot of sweat equity.

In its heyday, back when Martin Luther King, Jr. Boulevard was called West Broad Street, this building, erected in 1910, housed several African-American businesses, including a confectionary and a shoeshine shop. Shelley passed by this dormant building daily and imagined a way to breathe life into this all-too-oft-forgotten corner of the historic district.

Venus has a cozy, bohemian feel to it. There are several inviting parlors off the main rooms, with additional seating in the courtyard. On any given night, you'll find the most eclectic mix of folks around: from actuaries to artists, authors to attorneys. Their commonalities: a hip atmosphere, great conversation, and, of course, a love for wine.

38 Martin Luther King Jr. Blvd.
(912) 447-0901

Last Call

The next time you raise your glass, try offering one of these....

Here's to a long life and a merry one.
A quick death and an easy one.
A pretty girl and an honest one.
A cold beer — and another one!

Here's to you and here's to me,
Friends may we always be!
But, if by chance we disagree,
Up yours! Here's to me!

Here's to those who wish us well.
Those who don't can go to hell.

If you see my tombstone,
Please, don't pass it by.
Pour a drink on my grave,
'Cause I'll always be dry.

May you be in heaven a half hour
before the devil knows you're dead.

Here's to every man here,
May he be what he thinks himself to be.

Here's to our wives and lovers,
May they never meet!

May the Lord love us,
But not call us too soon.

If I had a ticket to heaven,
And you didn't have one, too,
I'd tear my ticket in half,
And go to hell with you!

Bibliography

Bailey, Cornelia Walker. 2000. *God, Dr. Buzzard and the Bo-lito Man: A Saltwater Geechee Talks about Life on Sapelo Island, Georgia.* New York: Anchor Books.

Berendt, John. 1994. *Midnight in the Garden of Good and Evil.* New York: Random House, Inc.

Bird, Stephanie Rose. 2004. *Sticks, Stones, Roots and Bones: Hoodoo, Mojo and Conjuring with Herbs.* St. Paul: Llewellyn Publications.

Caskey, James. 2005. *Haunted Savannah: The Official Guide-book to Savannah Haunted History Tour.* Savannah: Bonaventture Books.

Cobb, Al. 2003. *Savannah's Ghosts II.* Savannah: Whitaker Street Press.

Coffey, Tom. 1994. *Only in Savannah: Stories and Insights on Georgia's Mother City.* Savannah: Frederic C. Beil, Publisher.

Courlander, Harold. 1976. *A Treasury of Afro-American Folk-lore.* New York: Marlowe and Company.

Daise, Ronald. 1986. *Reminiscences of Sea Island Heritage.* Orangeburg, SC: Sandlapper Publishing, Inc.

Daiss, Timothy. 2002. *Rebels, Saints, and Sinners*. Savannah: Pelican Publishing Company.

DeBolt, Margaret Wayt. 1984. *Savannah Spectres and Other Strange Tales*. Virginia Beach, VA: The Donning Company.

Dick, Susan E. and Mandi D. Johnson. 2001. *Savannah: 1733 to 2000*. Charleston, SC: Arcadia Publishing.

Flexner, James Thomas. 1994. *Washington: The Indispensable Man*. (abridged) Boston, MA: Back Bay Books.

Fraser, Walter J. 2003. *Savannah in the Old South*. Athens, GA: University of Georgia Press.

Gamble, Thomas. 1923. *Savannah Duels and Duellists: 1733-1877*. Savannah: Review Publishing and Printing Co.

Georgia Writer's Project. 1940. *Drums and Shadows: Survival Stories Among The Georgia Coastal Negroes*. Athens, GA: University of Georgia Press.

Granger, Mary. 1997. *Georgia Writer's Project: Savannah's River Plantations*. Savannah, GA: Georgia Historical Society.

Henderson, Archibald. 1923. *Washington's Southern Tour*. Boston: Houghton Mifflin Co.

Jenkinson, Denis. 1959. *The Racing Driver: The Theory and Practice of Fast Driving*. Cambridge, MA: Robert Bentley.

Johnson, Wittington B. 1996. *Black Savannah*. Fayetteville: University of Arkansas Press.

Lane, Mills. 2001. *Savannah Revisited: History & Architecture, 5th Edition*. Savannah: The Beehive Press.

Pinckney, Roger. 1998. *Blue Roots: African-American Folk Magic of the Gullah People*. St. Paul: Llewellyn Publications.

Quattlebaum, Julian K. 1957. *The Great Savannah Races*. Athens, GA: University of Georgia Press.

Russell, Preston and Barbara Hines. 1992. *Savannah: A History of Her People Since 1733*. Savannah: Frederic C. Beil, Publisher.

Smith, Derek. 1997. *Civil War Savannah*. Savannah: Frederic C. Beil, Publisher.

Smith, Page. 1982. *Reflections on the Nature of Leadership*. Washington, D.C.: Anderson House.

Stevens, William Bacon. 1847. *A History of Georgia*. Reprint, Savannah, GA: Beehive Press, 1972.

Toledano, Roulhac. 1997. *The National Trust Guide to Savannah Architectural & Cultural Treasures*. New York: John Wiley & Sons.

Tucker, Windham, Kathryn, and Francis Lanier. 1987. *Thirteen Georgia Ghosts and Jeffrey*. Tuscaloosa, AL: University of Alabama Press.

Turnage, Sheila. 2001. *Haunted Inns of the Southeast*. Winston-Salem, NC: John F. Blair, Publisher.

Wheeler, Frank T. 2004. *The Savannah Races*. Charleston, SC: Arcadia Publishing.

Wilson, Annie Marie and Mandi D. Johnson. 1998. *Historic Bonaventure Cemetery*. Charleston, SC: Arcadia Publishing.

Yetman, Norman R., ed. 1970. *Voices for Slavery: 100 Authentic Slave Narratives*. New York: Holt, Rinehart, and Winston, Inc.

One for the Road

The saddest words ever composed,
Are these dismal four: "The bar is closed."